Mountain View

Maile-
You know _____!
love _____ you and that
this is crazy!
♡ Kim

Mountain View

A STORY OF GOD'S HEALING AND GRACE

Kim Penny

Fedd Books
P.O. Box 341973
Austin, TX 78734
www.thefeddagency.com

Published in association with The Fedd Agency, Inc., a literary agency.

Photo Cover Credit: Camille Davis

ISBN: 978-1-943217-61-8
eISBN: 978-1-943217-62-5

Printed in the United States of America
First Edition 15 14 13 10 09 / 10 9 8 7 6 5 4 3 2

To my Gami for persistently encouraging me to write my story down so that I could bring hope to others.

To all who came alongside me and walked this journey with me.

To Jon for becoming the embodiment of unconditional love. Only by God's grace were you able to love me through it all.

"My ears had heard of you but now
my eyes have seen you."

—Job 42:5

Table of Contents

Introduction

I had an almost-storybook childhood. I grew up on a 160-acre farm outside of Lawrence, Kansas, with a lake in my backyard, a beautiful prairie that bloomed with vibrant flowers each spring, plenty of forested area to play in, and land roaming with wildlife—ducks, geese, deer, coyotes, fish, frogs, turtles—you name it, we saw it. It was basically one giant playground for adults and children alike.

I was a very active and adventurous child. Being the youngest of three, I was continually trying to mimic and keep up with everything my older brothers and their friends were doing. We were constantly outside playing, whether it was football, basketball, or waterskiing on our lake. Everything we did was a competition or race of some kind.

Gymnastics was my very favorite, my passion. It didn't matter where I was—in my living room, my grandparents' living room, outside in the grass, on sidewalks, in public—I was always flipping upside down or walking on my hands. I was entertainment for my entire family . . .

My family. My mom, dad, and two brothers were all extremely loving and supportive, and our home was a revolving door of family and friends. We had solid Christian values, and life was pretty easy for all of us, despite normal daily stresses.

I say my childhood was "almost storybook" because it wasn't perfect. Beginning when I was ten years old, my family faced a series of trials that shook us to the core. First, our house was robbed. Thieves took just about everything and left us feeling scared and unsafe in our home. Not long after, two of my grandparents were hospitalized, one of whom died shortly after. And finally, the last and most traumatic blow was finding out that my dad had been diagnosed with ALS, Lou Gehrig's disease. My life, as I had known it, flipped upside down. My dad passed away two weeks prior to my junior year of high school, when I was only sixteen years old. His death was the first tragedy I'd ever known, and I've realized over time that it impacted me more deeply and made more of a mark on my life than I ever thought possible.

Despite having to move and switch school districts with only two years left of high school, God blessed me beyond measure both academically and athletically. I was asked to be captain of both my tennis team and cheerleading squad, I won multiple state medals in middle-distance running, and I was named Female Athlete of the Year. The biggest blessing came when, upon graduation, I was awarded an academic and athletic scholarship to the University of Nebraska. It was there where I met my husband who faithfully, through sickness and in health, has been by my side for the past fifteen years. We got married when we were only twenty and twenty-three years old and looked forward to a lifetime of adventure.

After a sky's-the-limit move to Durango, Colorado, to enjoy skiing, mountain biking, and exploring as young, active newlyweds, I experienced my second tragedy in life when I hit a tree snow tubing backcountry in the Colorado San Juan Mountains. Once Search and Rescue snowmobiled me to safety, I was Life-Flighted to a Level 1 trauma hospital where I began my long, long, *I-had-no-idea how long* journey of healing. That trauma hospital is where God began a major transformation in me. I began with broken bones, neurological damage, internal injuries, and crushed dreams. Today, fourteen years later, I have full mobility, a few races under my belt, my same incredible husband, precious twin girls, and a story to tell.

I don't want this to just be "my story," though. I don't care to simply tell you the details of my accident because everyone faces trials and hard times. What I *do* hope to do is encourage you in *your* struggle and in the often-long process of understanding and waiting on God's timing. I'm here to say I understand your impatience. I sympathize with your heartache. What has happened to you isn't necessarily fair, and it certainly isn't fun. And yet . . .

God is with you, and he's a performer of miracles.

I have known the Lord to be a father to the fatherless (Psalm 68:5), a comforter in times of trouble (Psalm 46:1), and a healer of heart, mind, body, and spirit (Jeremiah 17:14). He knows the cries of our hearts, and he cares to mend all that is broken. As you face your own adversities, may you find hope in this book and know that "though now for a little while you may have had to suffer grief in all kinds of trials, these have come so that the proven genuineness of your faith—of greater worth than *gold*, which perishes even though refined by fire—may result in praise, glory and honor when Jesus Christ is revealed" (1 Peter 1:6-7).

The Lord is mighty to save (Zephaniah 3:17) and eager to restore far more than you even think needs restoring. I invite you to have faith in the impossible and expect God to help and heal you and all those you love the most.

1.

The Accident

May 2007. After fifty miles of cycling and 6,000 feet of elevation gain, I felt like giving up. I wanted to stop pedaling, but I knew that at the top of the final climb I would reach the destination that only a few years earlier changed my life forever. The fifty-mile Iron Horse Bicycle Classic ended in Silverton, Colorado, but I had my eyes on a different prize. I was just 200 yards away from the top of Molas Pass.

My heart was pounding so hard it was resonating throughout my whole body. Everything was silent, except for the heavy breathing of other cyclists around me. The only thing running through my mind for the last three-and-a-half hours was the verse written on the back of my bike jersey, Isaiah 40:31: "But those who wait on the Lord shall renew their strength; they shall mount up with wings like eagles, they shall run and not be weary, they shall walk and not faint" (KJVA).

The scenery was breathtaking. Aspen and pine trees were everywhere, and patches of green grass popped through the melting snow packs. Best of all were the 360-degree views of the mountains. As I was biking up the windy mountain road, 14,000-foot peaks towered above me in every direction.

I had been waiting and training for this ascent for four years. My eyes welled with tears as the top grew closer. Memories of this area and the fight for my life began flashing through my mind, and suddenly, I couldn't control my thoughts or emotions. A burst of energy flooded my body with pent-up determination to reach the top. My husband, Jon, was by my side, just as he was the day of my accident. Just as he has been ever since.

Finally reaching the top, with tears streaming down my face, I looked around and noticed emergency vehicles, a Silverton ambulance, and a Flight for Life helicopter, all parked on call in case of an accident. The tears vanished and turned to laughter at the irony that the same vehicles that had pulled me, shattered and broken, off this mountain were here to greet me today in my triumph! I stepped off my bike, looked up at the bright blue Colorado sky, and praised God for healing my broken body and loving me enough to allow me this experience—this moment that fulfilled my heart's desire.

The Accident

My accident had happened in the middle of winter. It was now spring, four years later—a different season of the year and a different season of my life. As I stood on the mountaintop, I reflected back on all that had happened and all that God had seen me through.

Jon and I were forever changed by my accident on Molas Pass. Had God given us a choice as to whether or not we wanted to endure it and the trials that happened after, we certainly wouldn't have chosen the hard path. But his ways are not ours: "For my thoughts are not your thoughts, neither are your ways my ways, declares the Lord. As the heavens are higher than the earth, so my ways are higher than your ways and my thoughts than your thoughts" (Isaiah 55:8-9). In God's goodness and grace, he allowed the pain, the surgeries, the waiting, and the questions to increase my faith, produce maturity, and strengthen my relationship and dependence on him. I believe I am blessed: "Blessed is a man who perseveres under trial; for once he has been approved, he will receive the crown of life which the Lord has promised to those who love him" (James 1:12, NASB).

We took two photos at the top of Molas Pass: one with the ambulance and another with my husband and our bikes. At this point, it was all downhill to Silverton to finish the race.

* * *

Jon and I moved to Durango, Colorado, from Lawrence, Kansas, right after our wedding. Remember that active child I told you about? Picture me a little older but just as much of a risk-taker. I loved to ski, hike, ride bikes, and do all things outdoorsy. And Jon? He enjoyed it all too. We thrived outside. We lived to play. And in our early twenties, there wasn't much you could do to stop us.

On December 14, 2003, a little over a year after our first anniversary, God allowed the trajectory of our life to change. It was a Sunday, no different than any other, and we wanted to play in the snow. Durango still hadn't received any significant amount of snow in town. The ski resort was open, but we had our minds set on more adventure in an area at a higher elevation with more snow. We woke up early, went to church, and returned home to put on our snow gear and meet our friends. We were headed up to Molas Pass, a good hour-and-a-half drive north of Durango, to go backcountry snow tubing.

Jon and I had been sledding in this same area just a year earlier, but we thought we would increase the intensity and speed by bringing inner tubes this time. I was so excited—of all the new activities we had done over the past year, snow tubing was becoming a quick favorite. I had been praised the previous year for having incredible aerodynamics; I knew how to position myself in such a way to maximize my speed.

We took off on a long, winding drive, got to the top of the pass, unpacked our tubes and snowshoes, put on our goggles, ski jackets, gloves, and hats, and headed off back-country to find our hidden spot.

The sky was blue, and the sun was beating down on us as we hiked thirty minutes deep into the mountains making fresh tracks in three feet of powder. We took turns leading the group because the person in front does all the work creating the tracks. The leaders are the ones packing the snow down to make it easier for the rest of the group to hike behind. We stayed away from tree wells, which can be dangerous if you get too close. You can fall down into them and be buried by the snow. Finally, we made it to our destination. We were sweaty, out of breath, and ready for a fun afternoon of snow tubing.

It seemed like a safe-enough spot—clear of trees and a good quarter-of-a-mile run. Once you make it to the bottom, it takes thirty minutes to hike back up to the top because of the pitch of the hill, the depth of the snow, and the lack of oxygen at 10,000 feet. As we stood at the top, the first question was, "Who wants to go first?"

Our friend offered to be the guinea pig and jumped on the tube. He made it about thirty feet, the tube flew out from under him, and his ride was over. I decided I would show him up and go next because I knew I could do better than thirty feet. Jon and our three friends stood at the top as I sat on the tube, pulled my goggles down, and pushed off . . .

I picked up speed fast as I started on a natural ramp and immediately turned backwards. In my head, I was doing well. I was going fast, holding on tight, and picking up speed. As I was going backwards, though, my husband and friends could see what was going to happen next. They were screaming at me to jump, but I couldn't hear them. I was doing my own screaming—a different kind. I was laughing and yelling out of joy. They were screaming out of terror.

In an instant, and for no particular reason, my tube spun forward. I had a split second to make a decision. Jump? No, it was too late, and I was in a patch of trees. Even if I jumped, I was going to hit a tree, so I straightened my right leg to take the brunt of the impact. I hit the tree with the bottom of my foot going approximately thirty miles an hour, and it spun me to the right and a halting stop.

As I was lying on my back in the snow with my head pointed down the mountain and my legs above me, I watched as the tube continued its way to the bottom. My first thought was, *Wow! That was a close one. That could have been really bad!* Then I looked up the mountain at my legs and noticed that my right leg had been completely hyper-extended and looked like it was about three feet longer than my left leg. I also recognized that I had lost all feeling and movement in it.

As soon as I realized I had been injured, I started screaming, "I broke my leg! I broke my leg!" I looked up and saw my husband running down toward me. Our friends were at the top because one of them passed out at the sight and sound of what just happened. I was told it sounded like a gunshot when I hit the tree.

As soon as Jon reached me, he immediately started packing my leg in snow, which we found out later saved my life. Right away we thought my lower leg was going to be amputated—it didn't look salvageable. I accepted the fact that I may lose my lower leg and somehow found peace in that. I remember Romans 8:28 coming to my mind: "And we know that in all things God works for the good of those who love him, who have been called according to his purposes . . . "

Still, I lay in the snow thinking, "I may never run again."

I believe God, in his mercy and grace, protected me in that moment from knowing what was in store: how many surgeries I would have to endure (a total of fifteen), how much pain I would be in, how many hospital stays I would have, how long I would be on crutches, how many hours

I would spend in physical therapy, how much it would cost, how my appearance would change, and how I would have to relearn to walk and readapt to my everyday activities. Had I had known all those struggles, I may not have fought so hard for my life. Ignorance was bliss.

To this day, I believe God spared my life the instant my tube spun forward. He is the creator of life. If he wanted to take my life, he had the opportunity to right then and there. But he chose not to. When I was lying in the snow, I knew I was helpless and that God was in control. He gave me a peace and spoke to me. I knew I was going to live, and whatever path God was going to lay before me was my cross to bear. I needed to be strong, persevere, and trust that God knew best: "The Lord himself goes before you and will be with you; He will never leave you nor forsake you. Do not be afraid; do not be discouraged" (Deuteronomy 31:8).

Because God had given me the peace that I was going to be okay, I was not worried. I kept reassuring Jon that I felt fine. I was confident we were going to get help and that everything was going to be alright.

It was now mid-afternoon. We were in the middle of nowhere with no cell phone service and a good forty-five-minute hike from the car. Jon stayed with me while our three friends plowed their way through the snow back up to the car to call 911. We were alone for four hours.

I can't imagine everything that was going through Jon's head. I know he felt so helpless and guilty for having me in this position. He was thinking about how he was going to break the news to our families, and at the same time, trying to figure out how to get me off that mountain and to a hospital.

It was so quiet—almost deafening. We lay there in the snow and prayed, waiting for God to perform some type of miracle. Honestly, I think we were expecting an angel to appear. I remember thinking, "If there is ever an opportunity for a face-to-face encounter with God it is *now*." But nothing happened. We had to be still. Pray. Trust. Have faith.

It started to get dark, and when it gets dark in the mountains, it gets even colder. My lips were turning blue.

After a painfully long time of waiting, help appeared. Our friends came back with Search and Rescue on snowmobiles who had a sled to load me on and pull me off the mountain. Everyone breathed a sigh of relief. Now we were fighting time. It was getting colder, and a snowstorm was rolling in. Jon was pleading with Search and Rescue to fly a helicopter in, but the weather was getting bad, and they didn't know if there would be enough clearance to land. They straightened my right leg, realigned my body, placed my leg in a straight-leg brace, and loaded me onto the sled. Believe it or not, I still hadn't experienced a significant amount of pain up until this point. God had been protecting me by pouring out his grace as I waited for help.

Once I was on the sled, Search and Rescue attempted to pull me straight up the hill I had plummeted down, but the pitch was too steep and the snow too deep for the snowmobile. I remember thinking, *Finally, there is a rescue crew here to "save" me, and they can't get me out!* They sent another snowmobile around a different section of the mountain to see if there was an easier way out and then came back to tell us about an alternate route. Off I went behind a snowmobile, bundled up in a one-man sled, going what felt like twenty miles per hour around the mountain.

That's when the pain started to set in. I could feel every bump, and it felt like we hit a thousand of them! We would start to get stuck, but then I would hear the motor of the snowmobile rev up. We would slowly make progress up the hill, then around another corner, and up another hill, finally making it to the top. I was thanking God he brought help, yet I was nervous because the situation was not working out how I would have imagined. Nothing was easy. And everything hurt.

Meanwhile, as I was being snowmobiled out, my poor husband was running as fast as he could behind us. He didn't want to leave my side, but he also couldn't run as fast as the snowmobile. Every step he took, he sunk deeper into the snow, and all of a sudden, we were all out of his sight. Jon was all alone, afraid he wouldn't make it to the top before they loaded me into the ambulance and took off.

At the top of the pass, the Silverton ambulance was waiting for me, and I felt instant relief. The medics transferred me from the sled to the back of the ambulance, and just as they were getting ready to close the doors, Jon arrived and was able to ride with me. Snow was falling; it was now dusk.

Once we settled into the ambulance ride, my adrenaline stopped kicking in, and the pain increased—at first a little, and then *a lot*. It continued to escalate over the course of the trip, one excruciating stab after another. The ambulance crew wasn't authorized to administer any type of pain medication, so I would have to wait until I arrived at the hospital for relief.

A trip to the hospital from where I was would've typically taken about an hour and a half, but because of the bad weather and the icy, winding roads, it took about three hours instead. Despite my layers of coats, blankets, hats, and hand warmers, I was frozen after being on the mountain that long. Once I thawed out in the ambulance, the EMTs started unwrapping me to find out the extent of my injury. Then they started cutting my clothes off to get me ready for the transfer to the hospital.

We finally arrived at the hospital seven hours after I hit the tree, and for the first time all day, things started moving quickly. The pain had reached a level I didn't think was humanly possible. I was taken immediately to get X-rays of my leg. Nothing looked very bad initially—no broken bones, but definite knee damage. Then they X-rayed my pelvis, and we found our main culprit: a shattered pelvis. A new sense of urgency kicked in around the emergency room because a broken pelvis meant internal bleeding, and mine had been bleeding for the past seven hours. Packing my leg and body in snow had saved my life because it slowed the bleeding. Doctors told me that had this happened in a warmer climate, and it had taken that long to get help, I would have died.

The doctors tried to get an IV started, but I had lost too much blood and was dehydrated. Jon and I prayed as the hospital staff poked and prodded. Finally, they found a vein that worked and immediately gave me two units of blood (roughly 20 percent of the total amount of blood in my body) and my first dose of pain medicine. Now that I knew I had more than a broken leg and my injuries were much more serious than I initially believed, I asked the nurse if I would ever run again. She avoided the question and tried to comfort me, so I asked someone else. They avoided the question as well. I knew it was bad and that I was in for some major recovery time, but again, God protected me from knowing what the future would hold.

My injuries required a Level 1 trauma center, and because this was a Level 3, I needed to be transferred to a different facility. Doctors told us that a surgeon at St. Anthony's Central Hospital in Denver specialized in reconstructive pelvis surgery, and they could Life Flight me there. I would arrive in thirty minutes, rather than the normal six hours by car. Unfortunately, after talking to the pilot, though, they told us the weather was too bad between Durango and Denver, and they didn't think it was safe to fly. The medical team thought it would be best to send me to Albuquerque, New Mexico, even though the hospital in Albuquerque was a Level 2 facility and wouldn't offer the same level of treatment Denver could.

God, why are you allowing everything to go wrong? It was the first time I questioned what was going on, but I couldn't help but wonder. Jon and I prayed, asking God to allow us to go to Denver. After the doctors had another conversation with the pilots, they decided that if we left immediately, we would have a short time frame where it would be safe enough to fly to Denver. Praise God! I felt his assurance once more.

Doctors weren't sure if Jon could fly on the jet with me. It was a small jet, and they thought adding an extra person might make the plane too heavy. But I couldn't stand the idea of flying by myself while my husband drove over icy mountain passes in the middle of the night. We prayed again, and the doctors decided they would allow Jon to travel with me. Another answered prayer. If only things had kept looking up . . .

2.

Hospital

You will keep in perfect peace those whose minds are steadfast, because they trust in you. Isaiah 26:3 was on my mind during the thirty-minute trip on the jet, which made the flight strangely peaceful. Somehow I trusted God's plan and had already accepted the fact that my accident had happened. Plus, we were headed to the best hospital for the care I needed, and I had my husband next to me for support. I felt God's love and hand in the situation.

It was a quick flight; it felt like as soon as we took off, we were coming in for a landing at the Denver Airport. When we arrived, the medical team told Jon and me that we would have to separate for a short amount of time. Jon would need to take a cab to the hospital, while I was transported by helicopter. I kissed my husband and told him I would see him soon.

I remember looking out the window the entire time I

was in the helicopter. I was trying to keep my eyes on Jon's cab because I didn't want to be left alone. I knew I needed his support, and he needed mine. It was night, and the whole city was lit. We flew over the Broncos' stadium and then headed in for a landing on the rooftop of the hospital. I was taken off the helicopter and directly to ICU.

If you have ever experienced a Level 1 trauma center ICU, you know it is very busy. Within thirty minutes of arriving, there was another helicopter that brought in a family from another nearby town. They weren't as fortunate. It was a car accident—one person had died on the scene, and the other family member who was being flown in wasn't given a very high chance of survival. That put everything in perspective very quickly. *Thank you, God, for sparing me.* I prayed. *I don't know why you chose to spare my life, but you did. Thank you!*

Soon after I arrived, Jon pulled up to the hospital and was back by my side. My operation wouldn't take place immediately. The pelvis specialist wasn't readily available for my surgery, so another doctor put my leg in traction first. Before they put my leg in traction, the nurse gave us a quick *Cliff Notes* version of what traction was—a rod through my femur, right above my knee—and told Jon he might want to leave the room.

When I woke up from the sedative, I had a metal rod through my leg, which was connected to a pulley system of weights hanging off the end of my bed. It might as well have been a medieval torture device! I later found out that traction would prevent my femur from pulling up into my pelvis causing additional damage. *Okay, God,* I thought. *I wasn't expecting that. I can't imagine what the scar will look like when they take that thing out!* It was the first time I had thought about what my injury would do to the way I looked. As a twenty-one-year-old female, I was fairly concerned about my appearance and still hopeful that I could walk out of my injury without a scar.

It was midnight, time for this day to be over . . .

* * *

To my surprise, my mother was there when I woke the next morning. When she had heard the news from Jon the night before, she stayed up all night packing and finding the first flight out of Kansas City. Even though I was married and thought I was independent, I was still only twenty-one. The sight of my mom was comforting.

That day, the phone calls started. We called my brothers, other family members, and friends. Everyone was shocked and started praying for us. The day was also full of medical testing to find out the extent of my injuries. Obviously, my pelvis was shattered. We knew I had a knee injury since it was hyperextended at the time of my accident, and I still didn't have feeling or movement in my leg, so doctors assumed there was nerve damage as well. They needed to do an MRI to find out exactly what was wrong with my knee. The nurses gave me a lavender-scented eye mask to help me relax as I laid in the machine for an hour and a half. Once the testing was complete, they took me back to my hospital bed to wait for the results.

It turns out, I had completely torn my PCL, had possible tears in my ACL and LCL, a torn meniscus, and some significant nerve damage. I had also possibly severed my peroneal nerve and broken my tibia plateau. My knee would require surgery.

OK, I thought to myself. *Two surgeries—one for my pelvis and one for my knee. I can handle that. God will give me strength* . . . The verse Isaiah 40:28-29 came to my mind in those moments: *Do you not know? Have you not heard? The Lord is the everlasting God, the Creator of the ends of the earth. He will not grow tired or weary, and his understanding no one can fathom. He gives strength to the weary and increases the power of the weak.*

Next was taking a look at my sciatic and peroneal nerve. After the testing was complete, I found out that when my pelvis was crushed, I damaged my sciatic nerve, and the areas I would experience the most noticeable damage would be my gluteus maximus as well as my hamstring. It turns out, when you damage nerves, they kind of "spaz out" initially, so it is hard to determine the long-term effects of the damage. I knew at that time, though, that I may lose the ability to use my upper leg, and I had already lost feeling there.

Then doctors performed an EMG on my peroneal nerve, which revealed no response. I hadn't had any feeling from my knee down since the accident. I had no feeling or movement in my foot. I could barely push my toes down, but that was it. I couldn't pull my foot up or move it side to side. Again, I was told that nerves were sensitive and that there was a chance they might start to work again after a few days, months, or maybe even a couple years. Overall, though, there was no clear answer regarding the extent of my injuries.

Finally, upon completion of a full-body exam, I knew that I would require one surgery for my pelvis, one surgery on my knee, and may never be able to use my right leg from my waist down again. Still looking for answers and security, I asked the neurologist if I would ever run again, and he side-stepped the question. Of course, only God knew the answer; I would need to continue trusting him. I was thankful to still be alive and knew he was in control. "So do not fear, for I am with you," I heard him reassure me. "Do not be dismayed, for I am your God. I will strengthen you and help you; I will uphold you with my righteous right hand" (Isaiah 41:10).

Before long, a new type of pain began to emerge. I had

been experiencing pain in my lower back and pelvis, and my upper leg was swollen to about five times its normal size. But now I was having burning pain in my *foot*, which I couldn't feel. The nurses gave me pain medication, but it wasn't touching this pain. What was this? Why wouldn't it go away? *Why am I feeling pain in an area of my body that I can't even feel?*

It turns out, the pain was a phantom nerve pain— something to this day I still can't figure out how to manage. The pain added insult to injury. *God, you took away the feeling in my foot and replaced it with a constant burning pain? It feels like my foot is on fire and being stung by a swarm of bees at the same time! How is that fair?* I heard the Lord quickly respond: "For by grace you have been saved through faith; and that not of yourselves, it is the gift of God" (Ephesians 2:8). It was all I needed to hear. Suddenly, my body began to relax.

I was nearing the end of my third day in ICU, which meant it was time for my first operation. Despite being an extremely active child, I had never broken anything or had a surgery of any kind. It was a new experience. The surgeon was on the night shift, so I went in at three o'clock in the morning. I was nervous, which resulted in my being acutely aware of everything going on around me. There were still a lot of unknowns when it came to my pelvis injury. We didn't know how much damage the surgeon would find once he was actually looking at the broken bone or how much reconstruction he would have to do. Jon and I weren't ready to have children, but we did want a family down the road. This surgery could jeopardize our ability to have children. All we could do was pray for God to direct the surgeon and knit me back together the way I was intended to be.

When I woke up from surgery, the doctors gave me good news—it went well! Praise God! They used a foot-long metal plate and ten screws to put everything back in place and told me that where the break was shouldn't interfere with bearing children in the future. That was great news, but my flesh started to surface again. I was initially worried about what the scar would look like when they took my leg out of traction. Now I had a whole new kind of scar to worry about. I had an eighteen-inch scar from the surgery that was held closed with staples; I felt like Frankenstein.

The days were long in the hospital, and I was completely bedridden. Any time I needed to move, I had to call the nurses to roll me to one side or the other. They used pillows to put my body in different positions and help make me more comfortable. I was feeling more pain after the surgery than I felt before, which was unfathomable because before the surgery, I told the doctors that my pain was a 10 on a scale of 1-10. What would I consider this now—a *15*? The pain medicine the nurses were authorized to administer wore off long before they were allowed to give me another dose. I also had a catheter and was given an incredible amount of laxatives to counteract the pain medicine.

The longer I lay in bed, the more anxious I became. Thankfully, we had friends drive up from Durango to show their support, and they brought Christian music. Listening to it soothed me. My mom would also sit and read Scripture, and that put me at ease. When I wasn't listening to music or hearing God's Word, though, I went crazy. I wanted to jump out of bed and run out of the hospital, but I couldn't even move in bed without someone's assistance. *I was known for being a tomboy.* I thought to myself. *My entire identity was in being athletic. Now what have I become? I can't even roll over!*

Toward the end of my two-week stay, I started working with occupational therapists. They gave me equipment and taught me how to sit up by using the assistance of a strap hanging down from the top of my bed, then how to swing my legs over the side of the bed, and finally, how to stand up with a walker. The littlest things were enough to do me in, and I would have to lie back down in order to build strength and try it again in another few hours. I was exhausted, but it felt amazing to stand upright for the first time!

Hospital

Once I built up enough strength, the therapists would have me sit up and use the walker to make my way over to the oversized chair in my room. I was non-weight-bearing on my right leg for the next three months, so all the strength was coming from my left leg. I used all my energy just to keep my right leg from touching the ground. The day before I left the hospital, I could pull myself out of bed and use the walker to move about thirty feet down the hallway. I was thankful to be making progress, but I knew it would be a long road to recovery.

God answered another prayer when I was released from the hospital before Christmas. I wasn't cleared to travel back to Durango because the doctors were afraid there was too much risk in developing a blood clot with a six-hour drive, and they didn't even want me on a plane, but we had friends who lived in Denver and were out of town visiting family over Christmas. They offered their house as a place for us to stay until I was given permission to leave the area. I was released from the hospital on December 23rd.

I can't put into words how excited I was to leave the hospital. One day there feels like a week, so when you are there for two weeks, it feels like three-and-a-half months! My mom brought me clothes that fit over my braces, and for the first time, I was able to take off the hospital gown and put on regular clothes. I was starting to feel slightly human again. The nurses came in, I signed the release papers, and they cut the hospital band off. I was finally free! The hospital staff escorted me out in a wheelchair, and when I reached the front door of the hospital and went outside for the first time, I cried. The sun was beating down, and the wind was gently blowing over my face as I closed my eyes to soak it all in. I felt so grateful and blessed in that moment. My life had changed forever, and I had a long road ahead, but I felt *normal*.

Jon's parents pulled the car around, and it took three people to pick me up and place me in the front seat of the Suburban. Jon, his parents, and my mom all piled into the car, and off we headed to our friends' house. The drive was exhilarating. I had been immobile for so long that the car ride felt like I was riding in a racecar.

When we arrived at the townhome, we noticed there was a large flight of stairs to reach the front door. On to the next challenge: getting me inside. I had barely been moving on my own with a walker, and that had been restricted to level surfaces; even then, my balance was questionable. Plus, for safety purposes, I had to wear a belt with someone walking behind me to make sure I didn't fall. There was no way I was going to be able to get inside the house on my own.

By this point, every time an obstacle crept up, I just laughed at God because I knew he was teaching me to trust him. He knew these stairs were going to be there, and he wasn't about to make it easy on us. We all just laughed when we pulled up to the house, and Jon looked at me and said, "I guess we will have to carry you in!" To this day, I am still not sure what happened next, or how I reached the top, but somehow, Jon and his dad managed to drag me up the stairs through the front door and plop me down on the couch without hurting me. I was exhausted! It had been an eventful day, but I was happy. I was lying on a couch instead of a hospital bed. I was in the middle of a beautiful living room with Christmas decorations, and Christmas Eve was the next day. I felt blessed.

I received many Christmas gifts from the hospital: a raised toilet seat, a three-foot-long shoe horn, a drop-foot brace, a straight-leg knee brace, a stretchy band I could put on my foot to move my leg, a wound-care kit, and a three-foot claw that allowed me to grab items not within my reach when I was lying down. Not exactly what I had wished for, but I was thankful to be out of the hospital and able to spend Christmas with my family. Besides that, I was more thankful to celebrate Christmas that year than any other because the meaning of Christmas truly hit home. I had always celebrated the birth of our Savior, Jesus, but that year the thankfulness of having a Savior who cleansed me from *my* sins was more meaningful than ever because I had just come face-to-face with my own mortality. Before my accident, I was young and felt inde-structible; I certainly didn't think I would have to face the idea of my own death so early in life. But my accident was a wake-up call that made me so much more grateful that my sins had been washed clean and forgiven. Jesus had come into this world and died to save me! I realized that Christmas that the gift of eternal life is the only thing that truly matters, and I was humbled to know I didn't have to do anything to earn it. *For the wages of sin is death,* Romans 6:23 echoed in my mind. *But the gift of God is eternal life in Christ Jesus our Lord.*

Had I had died on the mountain, I would be in heaven today celebrating with my Lord and Savior, but that Christmas I knew that because I was still alive, God had a purpose for my life. Yes, there would be more pain and surgery and waiting, but God wanted me to enjoy him here on earth amidst it all. And he had good things in store for me. "The thief comes only to steal and kill and destroy," John 10:10 says. "I came that they may have life, and have it abundantly" (NASB).

3.

Surgery

I celebrated Christmas with Jon and my mom over a delicious home-cooked meal, which was such a treat after eating hospital food for as long as I had. We watched *It's a Wonderful Life* and held our own church service on Christmas Day. I was feeling rested and anticipated the road to recovery.

Jon and my mom had become full-time caretakers. I slept on the couch while Jon slept on the floor next to me. He was far more concerned about me than I was about myself. He took my temperature, watched the clock to see when medication was due, and gave me shots in my stomach to keep my blood from clotting since I was immobile. The shots hurt him more than they hurt me; he hated having to cause me more pain.

On December 26th, I woke up and didn't feel well. We couldn't figure out why I wasn't getting better—at this point, it had been over two weeks since my accident had occurred. *I should be getting better, not worse!* I thought to myself. Every time I stood up, I felt like I might pass out. I was still taking laxatives, but they weren't working. The only thing in my stool was blood. We had called the hospital before, and they had said that could be normal for my type of injury, but this time when they asked me to take my temperature, it was 106. Something needed to be done immediately! The only obstacle was figuring out how to get me out the front door and down the stairs to the car; I was fading quickly. The room was spinning, and I had no energy. Jon somehow loaded me onto his back and carried me down the stairs, and off we rushed back to the hospital.

When we arrived in the emergency room, the first thing the hospital staff did was strap another hospital band on me. *Great. There goes my freedom,* I thought. The nurses took my vitals and drew blood. I waited in a hospital bed as they came back to give me the results of what they found in the blood test: my white blood cell count was at 20,000. A normal reading would typically be around 5,000. Diagnosis: I had a bad infection. Next, we needed to find out what was causing the infection, so off I went for more testing. The first test they did was a barium CT scan—basically, I had to drink a full glass of a thick white chalky formula that I choked down and then have a CT scan. Once the test was complete, the doctors took me up to another hospital room to wait for the results. At this point, I had received antibiotics and pain medicine, so I was feeling better, and because I was feeling better, I wasn't as anxious about the results. After all, God had spared my life on the mountain and brought me this far. How much worse could it really get?

Jon planned to stay with me that evening in the room. My room didn't even have a chair, though, so he planned to sleep on the hard tile. My mom was offered a room at the Ronald McDonald charity house, so she kissed me good night and was headed out when a doctor came in with the results from my test earlier. He was not very friendly, probably because he was about to deliver bad news. He simply walked in and said, "You have a tear in your rectum, which has caused e-coli to infect your blood stream. If we don't do an operation in the next thirty minutes to give you a colostomy, you will die." And then he turned around and walked out of the room.

Seriously God?! Are you kidding me?! I was screaming in my head. Whatever calm and composure I'd found was now lost. We were all shocked. The doctor didn't even take the time to explain what a colostomy was, not that he needed to. Unfortunately, I already knew. My mom tried to comfort me with the idea of what it would be like to have one and how many people live full lives without any restrictions, but I didn't know what to think. I was trying to process all the information at one time. My options were to have the operation or die, and apparently, according to the doctor, I had only thirty minutes to make a decision. Of course, I would have the surgery.

As if I hadn't already lost enough self-confidence, here I was, newly married, and I had a large scar where they had put the rod through my femur and an eighteen-inch scar down my pelvis. Now I was going to have a poop bag too?! *My husband didn't sign up for this when he chose to marry me!* I thought to myself. Sure, he said, "for better or for worse, in sickness and in health," but did he ever picture this? Jon might have expected to deal with something similar to this after we grew old together, but *now? After only one year of marriage?*

The clock on the wall was directly across from my hospital bed just taunting me. The doctor said thirty minutes to live, and fifteen minutes had passed without any sign of a doctor or nurse. I was angry. I was scared. I was confused. I was faced with death again, and this time it seemed within someone's control. But there was nothing I could do, nowhere I could go, and no one there to fix my problem. God was the only one I could turn to, but even he seemed far away. I reached a breaking point. Trembling in fear and screaming in my head, I asked, *So God, are you just going to let me lie here and die after everything you've already brought me through? Don't you love me? Am I not your child? How can you do this to your child—especially since I have been obedient to you?! I have made good decisions in my life, and I have been faithful. Why do you wish to cause me such pain?*

I couldn't believe I was back in a hospital bed, facing death at worst and a poop bag at best. The only thing on my mind was God. I was, at the same time, questioning my faith and also verifying that it was real. What else could I cling to? My life was hanging in the balance—once again, God could choose whether or not he wanted to spare me.

I lay there as Jon and Mom prayed over me and read Bible verses. It was the only thing that calmed my nerves, as well as theirs, and reminded me of God's faithfulness amidst my confusion. "Do not be anxious about any-thing," I struggled to embrace. "But in every situation, by prayer and petition, with thanksgiving, present your requests to God. And the peace of God, which transcends all understanding, will guard your hearts and your minds in Christ Jesus . . . " (Philippians 4:6-7). Slowly but surely, God poured a steady stream of peace over me. Then he brought in a team of medical professionals to roll me off to surgery.

My surgery was at night, so I woke up in my hospi-tal room the next morning. The doctors told me that not only had they given me a colostomy, but they also cut back into my incision where I had my pelvis surgery to clean out the area and disinfect it. It turns out, when you have an infection, the antibiotics can clear out any infection in your bloodstream, but if you have foreign objects in your body (like my metal plate and screws), there is not a lot you can do to guarantee that the hardware won't carry the bacteria. They performed what is called irrigation and debridement (I&D) surgery in addition to the colostomy surgery. When the doctors left my bedside, I was nervous about looking at my pelvis and abdomen to see what type of collateral damage I would find.

It wasn't something I could avoid, but I at least wanted to wait for Jon to be with me before I took a peek. When he was there with me, I lifted my hospital gown and couldn't believe I was looking at myself. *This was my stomach and my pelvis?* I had a plastic bag connected to my lower intestine that was rerouted to the left side of my belly button and filled with loose stool. I had an incision from three inches above my belly button all the way down to the bottom of my pelvis, which intersected with my other incision where they reopened my eighteen-inch scar from my pelvis surgery. And of course, all the incisions were held closed with staples. If I didn't feel like a monster before, I really felt like one now! In addition, I had three drains inserted into my abdomen that slowly filled with drainage from the surgery. I didn't think it could get worse, but it did.

After having some alone time with Jon, a nurse came

in to show me how to use my new contraption. She explained how to use the bag and how to take it on and off and clean it. I was overwhelmed. It was difficult to follow her demonstration because I was still trying to process the fact that this was my new reality. Just days before I had been home celebrating *Christmas!* As soon as she finished her instructions, an infectious disease doctor entered my room and informed me that I would need to have a PICC line inserted, which would stay in place for the next six months because oral antibiotics were not strong enough to fight the type of infection I had. More bad news, and on to the next procedure . . .

A specialist came into the room, and everyone had to clear out for sanitary reasons. The specialist inserted a small white catheter into my left arm at my elbow and took it all the way up the vein until it dumped right into my heart. This allowed the IV antibiotics to go straight to my heart and pump through my body more quickly. *This was not what I signed up for!* I continued to think to myself. I had all sorts of contraptions hanging off me between the drains from the surgeries, the colostomy bag, and now a PICC line. Doctors told me I would need to stay in the hospital for another couple of weeks because they needed to do more irrigation and debridement surgeries to be sure the plate and screws weren't infected. *Great . . .*

The next thing on the schedule to look forward to, right

after I woke up from surgery, experienced my colostomy bag, and had a PICC line inserted, was to have another surgery that evening. I couldn't see the end in sight and knew I couldn't control my outcome, so I decided not to fight. I let go of all control. Off I went for another surgery.

I didn't fair so well when I woke up this time. My body had been through a lot and was being pushed to the limit. Even though it wasn't as invasive of a surgery, doctors still had to cut back into my pelvis incision for a third time and re-staple it closed. There was concern when I woke up because I had lost a lot of blood. I was given four units of blood over the next twenty-four hours, which was 40 percent of the total amount in my body. I still had one more irrigation and debridement surgery to go, and during this last surgery the plan was to place antibiotic beads directly on the hardware to ensure the site would stay clear of infection. Doctors told me that once my pelvis healed, because of the amount of infection I had in my body, I would now need to have surgery to *remove* the plate and screws. That way, if I were to ever have an infection in the future, it could be treated with antibiotics.

The doctors had originally planned to do the final I&D surgery the following day, but after seeing the poor condition I was in, they made the decision to let me rest before putting me under again. The extra recovery time did help me build strength, but it also caused extreme anxiety. I had done a pretty good job of accepting everything that had happened to me up until this point, but I was beginning to feel in over my head. I had been a tough girl with a high pain tolerance and not much of a complainer, but I didn't know how much more I could physically endure. I questioned whether or not I could handle another surgery. Two days later, I went in for my final I&D. The doctors cut into my pelvic incision for a fourth time, placed antibiotic beads on the hardware, and stapled me shut one last time.

Over the next week, I was poked, prodded, and taken at all times of the night to run different tests. I also worked with occupational and physical therapists and was given a crash course on how to use crutches because when I would arrive home, we lived in a three-story townhome. I wouldn't be able to climb stairs with a walker.

Finally, the day came when I would be released from the hospital. Because of how fragile my health was, we decided it would be best to stay in a local hotel for the next month to make sure my health was stable before we headed all the way back to Durango. Just like the first time I left the hospital, I put my own clothes on, threw the hospital gown on the chair, and signed the release documents. As the hospital band was cut off, I felt the sense of freedom run through me again. Outside, joy rushed over me as I sat in the wheelchair with the sun beating down and the wind blowing across my face. I breathed a sigh of relief that I was able to put another hospital stay behind me. Jon helped me into the car, and we headed to the hotel.

Just like at Christmas, the hospital sent a few additional items home with me. Included in my gift bag were a set of crutches, colostomy supplies, and a plethora of wound-care items. This time I also got regular hospital visitors! Nurses stopped by the hotel regularly to help us as we adapted to changing my colostomy bag and administering IV antibiotics into my PICC line. Probably the biggest blessing of all was that I was finally able to take a real shower for the first time since my accident occurred. I had to wrap half of my body in trash bags and plastic wrap to keep the incisions from getting wet (which could cause more infection), but I didn't care. It was the most incredible feeling to finally be *clean*!

Our stay at the hotel was the first time in over a month that I had been alone with Jon. The first night we ordered a pizza and watched a movie—*it was wonderful*. I had missed the simple things. I was finally able to sleep in the same bed with him for the first time since the accident occurred too; it was so comforting to have him next to me. We had a few trial-and-errors with the colostomy bag and actually named my intestine, "Stinky Stoma." God gave us joy and laughter in those days and allowed us to make the best out of a bad situation as we simply enjoyed being around each other. Every moment Jon and I had together was one more moment we wouldn't have been able to experience had I not made it off the mountain. We took advantage of every second.

I was becoming fairly comfortable on my crutches, so one day Jon and I decided to go on a field trip because we were getting cabin fever. I was so excited to go do something—*anything*—that didn't revolve around monitoring my health! We arrived at an outdoor amphitheater, and my stomach filled with butterflies. I was nervous to be out in public. I used the crutches to make my way down to the theater, and as I did, I realized how injured I really was. It took thirty minutes just to crutch to the bottom because of all the breaks I had to take along the way to catch my breath and regain strength. I knew I was weak and had lost a lot of strength, but this was ridiculous. I began dreading the long journey of healing I had before me because just this one trek down had taken so much out of me.

What made things worse was that there were little kids playing tag and athletes running stairs all around us. My dread suddenly became bitterness as I wished I could be like them. I was envious of the athletes working out and children playing because that is what I would have been doing had I not been hurt. Unfortunately, our happy outing had quickly turned into a reality check. Jon and I made it back to the car, and then I broke down in tears. I felt completely hopeless. How would I ever recover to the point of where I was prior to the accident?

That day at the amphitheater was a real turning point for me. I had been so focused on simply *surviving* my accident that I hadn't really faced the reality of a changed life and what it would be like in the "real world." How would I cope? What was life really going to look like? Amidst all of my questions, fear of "the worst" surfaced.

> *Doctors told me there was no guarantee that the e-coli infection would ever completely clear my system. They said it could lay dormant and then come back in five to ten years. What if it does? What if the blood from my six transfusions gets contaminated, and I develop AIDS or hepatitis? What if doctors can't reverse the colostomy, and I have to live with it the rest of my life? What if my nerves never come back, and I lose the use of my leg? What if I am never able to have children? What if Jon leaves me because I am now a burden? What if I have brain damage or other health issues down the road because of all the medications and anesthesia I have been under? What type of health issues will I have when I am older?*

But wait. I had to stop myself. I had to remind myself of who God was, who I was, and how God had led me through trials before. My God was not God of "the worst." He was God of healing and triumph and help. And I was not a hopeless person. God had made me active and strong and full of love, not doubt. Slowly but surely, I began to shift my focus off myself and my current condition and onto how faithful God had been in my life. In the midst of everything that had happened, my own life had become the biggest testament to me and my greatest encouragement because I knew that God, in the midst of heartbreaking trials, never left me. When my family was robbed years ago, God provided comfort, safety, and restoration to us afterwards. When my father and grandmother died, he brought peace. God had always turned bad situations into good, directed my path, restored my strength, given me peace of mind, and provided for my daily needs.

"Do not worry about your life," Jesus tells those who follow him . . .

> [Do not worry about] what you will eat; nor for your body, as to what you will put on. For life is more than food, and the body more than clothing. Consider the ravens, for they neither sow nor reap; they have no storeroom nor barn, and *yet* God feeds them; how much more valuable you are than the birds! And which

of you by worrying can add a *single* hour to his life's span? If then you cannot do even a very little thing, why do you worry about other matters? Consider the lilies, how they grow: they neither toil nor spin; but I tell you, not even Solomon in all his glory clothed himself like one of these. But if God so clothes the grass in the field, which is alive today and tomorrow is thrown into the furnace, how much more will He clothe you? You men of little faith! (Luke 12:22-28, NASB)

Yes, my faith was wavering, and I was full of worry. But I couldn't shake the reality of how much God loved me anyway and how willing and able he was to provide for me. God had been so very real to me in my life up until this point, and he had blessed and matured me in countless ways. There was no way I could give up on him now and lose hope.

My glass was not half empty; it was half full. I knew God had big plans in store for my life and healing. I just needed to be obedient, trust, and take it one day at a time. He would do the rest.

"The Lord will fight for you," I heard deep in my soul. "You need only to be still" (Exodus 14:14).

4.

Home

Once we were given the clear by doctors to leave the Denver area, we loaded our things into the car and made our way through the windy mountain roads back to the southwest corner of the state. What a relief to finally be home—it was if I had been holding my breath for the past three months and just exhaled for the first time. When we walked in the front door, we were strangely greeted with a few wet moldy items from the day of the accident. It was an eerie reminder of what started this whole ordeal. So much had transpired from that day till this moment, it felt as if the accident had occurred a lifetime ago.

Once we unpacked the car and settled in, it was time to go to sleep. I was finally able to relax in my own bed, which was such a relief, but getting situated was an ordeal because I had to wear a straight-leg brace as well as a stiff ninety-degree foot brace. I could only sleep on my back with my right leg propped up on pillows. In addition to that, I had to make sure my PICC line was secure so that it didn't get tangled, and there was always a slight fear I might pop my colostomy bag if I were to accidently roll to my side. Regardless of all the obstacles, I was so thankful. I felt like the worst was behind me, and it would only get easier from there.

Here's a breakdown of our daily routine once I finally got settled at home: We'd wake up, and then Jon would help me change my bandages and colostomy bag and get dressed. Then he'd escort me down the stairs to the main living area, make breakfast for the two of us, hook me up to the IV antibiotics, give me a kiss, make sure I had a phone nearby, and head off to work. I wasn't allowed to leave the second floor of our house unless I called Jon before I started up a flight of stairs, and then after I made it to the top successfully, I would need to call him again. You could say he was a little overprotective, but rightly so after my trauma.

On the healing front, the doctors in Denver transferred my medical records to specific local doctors to monitor my progress. I also started to work with a physical therapist full time. My accident occurred between semesters during my college winter break, so I unfortunately had had to drop the classes I was enrolled in for the spring semester. This was discouraging for me because I only had three semesters left to earn my degree, and now, instead of attending class, I had a full-time job simply taking care of myself. Jon went back to work for his engineering firm as I sat at home waiting for people to come pick me up to take me to and from appointments.

Of all the transformations my body had gone through, the one that was the most intriguing had to be the colostomy bag—there really is no getting used to it! Because there aren't muscles around the stoma, you can't control what it does. Jon and I found that the best way to cope with the colostomy bag was just to laugh at it. The first Sunday after we arrived home, I felt up to going to church, and on the drive over told Jon that my biggest fear was that the colostomy bag would make a noise during the service. We both laughed but thought the chances were pretty low that something might actually happen. We walked into church and were greeted by so many wonderful friends who had been praying for us throughout our whole ordeal. We took our seats, and shortly after, the pastor asked us all to bow our heads in silence for prayer. As soon as it was dead silent in the church, my stoma let out a loud noise. I was *mortified!* My worst fear had just come true. Thankfully, there was a baby next to me in the pew, so I convinced myself that most people in the congregation would think it was the baby. Jon and I laughed the whole way home from church.

What a blessing our congregation had become. We hadn't been attending our particular church for very long, but we knew a few people because we had joined a small group. Plus, my accident had gotten some attention in the church, so people we didn't even know stepped up to help the new young couple who needed their church family. Volunteers did everything from cooking and cleaning to driving me around town to appointments. All the interaction drew us really close to the congregation and gave new meaning to Scriptures I'd always heard about church. "Even so the body is not made up of one part but of many," 1 Corinthians says.

> Now if the foot should say, "Because I am not a hand, I do not belong to the body," it would not for that reason stop being part of the body. And if the ear should say, "Because I am not an eye, I do not belong to the body," it would not for that reason stop being part of the body. If the whole body were an eye, where would the sense of hearing be? If the whole body were an ear, where would the sense of smell be? But in fact God has placed the parts in the body, every one of them, just as he wanted them to be. If they were all

one part, where would the body be? As it
is, there are many parts, but one body. (1
Corinthians 12:14-20)

How do people survive without Christian community? And how could anyone ever feel insignificant in the
church?

It wasn't just Christians who helped. I was humbled
when volunteers from our community stepped in too.
Neighbors came over to clean my house. People I hardly knew ran errands for me and encouraged me to rest.
Like a lot people, I find it really hard to accept help from
others. I had always been a do-it-yourself type of person,
so I found it difficult to sit on the couch and have others
take care of me. I would feel guilty and offer to take over.
But people gently urged me to relax and understand that
they felt blessed to use their gifts and help in some way. As
I swallowed more and more of my pride over time, God's
grace and mercy became ever more present.

I also became more aware of God's presence through
my quiet time at home. Having limited mobility was a
huge challenge for me because I hated sitting still, but it
forced me to spend time journaling and praying, which
ended up being so good for my soul. God used the time
to show me how little control I had over my life and teach
me that prior to my accident, I had been fairly prideful in

my independence. I had a false sense of security thinking
I had life figured out. Newly married, moving to a fun new
town, and purchasing our first home (ironically a three-story townhome!), we were living in what I considered to be
paradise. What could possibly go wrong? When life as we
knew it came to a halting stop, though, thinking of myself
and our circumstances was anything but comforting. God
brought my gaze back to him and showed me that in my
weakness, he would make me strong: "Therefore, in order
to keep me from becoming conceited, I was given a thorn
in my flesh, a messenger of Satan, to torment me." Paul
writes in Scripture . . .

> Three times I pleaded with the Lord
> to take it away from me. But he said to
> me, "My grace is sufficient for you, for
> my power is made perfect in weakness."
> Therefore I will boast all the more glad-
> ly about my weaknesses, so that Christ's
> power may rest on me. That is why, for
> Christ's sake, I delight in weaknesses, in
> insults, in hardships, in persecutions, in
> difficulties. For when I am weak, then I
> am strong. (2 Corinthians 12:7-10)

No, what had happened to me was not fun; honestly,

it was practically tormenting. But the Lord had me in his hand, and he had not given up on me.

I saw a different specialist every day. The orthopedic doctors were monitoring my pelvis incision and my knee. The staples had been removed from my pelvis since the last surgery, but one area hadn't healed. There was a large hole that looked like a deep abyss. In addition to the hole, some of the screws that had been used during my pelvis surgery were starting to push to the surface of my skin as the bone healed, so there was constant rubbing that occurred around my waist line. It was disturbing to see and feel the top of the screws. Again, because of the infection, there was already a plan to have the plate and screws removed in six months, but until that time, I would have to live with the discomfort. I would visit the infectious disease doctor once a week to change the dressing around my PICC line and have my blood drawn to make sure the antibiotics were keeping the infection under control.

Physical therapy easily became the highlight of my week. Because of my sports background, being in a gym with a trainer made me feel at home; it was familiar territory. And I loved my physical therapists. They were so positive, encouraging, and supportive that I actually looked *forward* to being around them. My team almost singlehandedly allowed me to maximize my recovery. I would not be where I am today without them.

My first appointment was spent assessing my injury to acquire a baseline so we could measure my progress over the next few months. The initial test results were not surprising. The left side of my body was strong and functioning—completely normal. The right side of my body from my waist down was a different story. I had a significant amount of atrophy. (Jon lovingly called my quad muscle my "uno.") My hamstring and glut had no response to the e-stim machine, which basically acts like the nerves in your body; it shocks the muscles and nerves, sending signals to contract. We measured where the loss of feeling occurred and traced it down my leg with a black magic marker. Then, once a week, we would do an assessment to see if any of the feeling came back. It was a big deal to have even the slightest bit of feeling or movement return because it meant there was still life in the damaged nerve. And life in the nerve meant that there was a possibility for that nerve to recover, leading to muscle strength and, ultimately, more use of my leg.

Physical therapy wasn't without its challenges, though. What I considered the simplest of exercises were complicated, painful, and almost impossible to do. Because I was non-weight bearing for three months, I did most of my exercises lying on a table. I would spend hours doing leg lifts with assistance. Lying on my back, if my leg went past a ninety-degree angle I would immediately lose all control and have to either block my face or grab my leg with my hands to keep it from hitting me in the face. I had zero use of my hamstring. After I did ten leg lifts on my back, I would then roll to my left side and try to lift my right leg up and down, again with assistance. The trainer had to stabilize my leg for me, or it would flail out of control similarly to how it did when I was lying on my back. Next, I would roll to my stomach to repeat the exercise, which was the most frustrating position for me. It seemed so easy—I could do 1,000 leg lifts like this with my left leg, but I couldn't even do one with my right. The trainer would have to *help* me lift my leg up and down, when normally I would have just mentally sent the signal from my brain down to my leg and tell it to contract and lift up. I wanted to cry. *How could I not lift my own leg?*

After a few sets of leg lifts, I would then work on leg extensions and hamstring curls. This meant I was able to take the straight-leg brace off, something I hadn't been able to do until this point. Having my brace off gave me a new sense of freedom because it gave me the ability to bend my knee again. The leg extensions were an encouragement—my quad was weak and had limited nerve damage, but at least I had the ability to make the movement.

The leg curls were a different story because they required me to use primarily my hamstring, which I had no use of. I knew the therapist was doing everything he could to help me get muscle memory back and try to stimulate any type of nerve still there in my upper leg, but I felt so frustrated and defeated. I hated that I was being asked to do something I physically couldn't—it felt like salt being poured into my wound. It was as if the fact that I had lost all ability to use my leg was being rubbed in my face every time my therapist asked me to curl my leg behind me. I had to have 100% assistance to do this simple act.

Most of us go about our daily lives doing the simplest movements with our body. We don't even realize we are doing things like stretching our hamstrings or contracting our quadriceps. In the past I never would have thought twice about how my muscles and nerves interact with each other to create specific movement. I wouldn't have thought about how the *idea* of movement travels from my brain to the specific body part I am actually trying to *move*. When you feel it, though—when you experience *failure* in simply trying to move your body—you can't help but feel defeated.

Next, my therapist would ask me to sit on the table, and we would work on trying to strengthen the muscles in my foot and ankle. These exercises were just as devastating as the leg lifts. My therapist asked me to simply push my foot down. *OK, I can do that,* I thought. *There is a little movement. Success!* "Next, pull your foot up," he said. With those words, I went through the same frustration as with the hamstring curls. I was mentally telling my foot to pull up, trying so hard my knuckles turned white as I gripped the table. My body would shake as I tried to will my foot up. But the end result was no movement. Then my therapist would ask me to move my foot from side to side. Again, nothing but pure frustration.

In order to build muscle mass, you have to contract the muscle. Unfortunately, because I was starting from scratch and unable to make muscles contract on my own, my only chance of building the muscle back up was to use a machine to make the muscle contract.

So after I was done with my exercises, my therapist would hook one e-stim machine up to my hamstring and glut and another to my shin muscle and foot to try and stimulate the muscles that weren't responding in order to have some contraction. Once I was unhooked from the e-stim unit, I would then have to ice down before I was free to leave. To make things even more fun, my therapist even gave me homework when I left, exercises I needed to do in the evenings. This cycle continued day in and day out.

I faithfully did everything I was asked to do, and thankfully, one day we encountered a major turning point. It was a Saturday morning, and Jon was helping me use the e-stim unit. We had it placed on my glut and hamstring, and for the first time in over four months, when we turned the unit on, we saw movement. We couldn't believe it! We had been praying that God would bring my strength back. This was a small glimmer of hope that the nerves might not be completely damaged in my upper leg and that I might be able to build the muscles back up, ultimately giving me more mobility and independence in my daily life. Again, there was a long road ahead, but for the first time, we saw real progress when it came to building back strength. Praise God!

After that milestone, Jon and I began to embrace the "baby steps" of my recovery and learned to laugh a bit more. Because I knew I had the ability to strengthen my leg over time, the fact that I lost control when it went past a ninety-degree angle became funny. As I slowly gained strength, it turned into a game to see how much I could control it. I would lie on my back and lift my leg up in the air. It would wobble around in the air and fly out of control toward my face. My leg was like a rag doll—I was the most flexible I had ever been! My injury became full-time entertainment as Jon and I were learning daily how to manage it.

Thankfully, I was also starting to feel more confident with my ability to move on crutches, and I had built up enough strength to manage daily tasks. *Now, if only I didn't have to depend on others to travel,* I thought to myself. I honestly felt like I could drive safely, but there were a few minor setbacks: I didn't have any feeling in my right foot, I couldn't pull up to let off the gas, and I couldn't move my foot from the gas pedal to the brake. I would need to learn how to drive with my left foot. At a routine doctor appointment, I asked for, and was granted permission, to do just that. I was so ecstatic—I felt like a teenager who had just been given a learner's permit! When Jon returned home from work that evening, we headed to a large empty parking lot so I could practice driving with my left foot. I was a little jerky at first but adapted quickly to this new style of driving. As soon as Jon felt comfortable riding as a passenger, he gave me the go-ahead to drive all the way home. Another sense of freedom—I could now get around on my own. Things were continuing to look up. For the first time, I was able to truly envision independence in my future.

5.

Confusion

I often refer to my accident and recovery as an obstacle course. It wasn't just full of ups and downs; there were also hurdles and side-steps and slips and slides. Some of the most challenging parts about it all were actually some of the smallest snags along the way. Medical bills, for example. Though my physical recovery was starting to make real progress, medical bills were becoming my biggest headache.

As if it isn't shocking enough to go through a traumatic and life-changing accident, we were not prepared for the price tag that came along with it. After finally settling in at home and getting used to a new routine, the bills started rolling in. First a few, and then a *flood*. We were overwhelmed, to put it mildly. Considering the fact that Jon and I were newly married, we were pretty proud of how we budgeted our money. We had our monthly budget

set up on a spreadsheet, and we tracked—to the penny—
where our money went. We also made it a point to sit
down together at the end of each month to assess each
category to see where we could cut back and save a few
dollars. No matter how well we had mastered Budgeting
101, though, this was a whole new ballgame . . .

The Life Flight alone was $20,000. We quickly learned
what *in-network* and *out-of-network* insurance providers were.
We received multiple bills from different departments
within the hospital. Each surgery was billed separately
and consisted of one charge for the facility, one for the
team of surgeons, and another from the anesthesiologist.
I received bills from the radiology department, the pa-
thology department, the neurologist, etc. Of course these
departments and individuals deserve to be paid—they
earned every penny for the services they provided—but it
was crushing to suffer trauma and then face the reality of
how much that trauma cost. Two big blows.

One piece of good news about our medical bills—
if there was any—is that they gave me something to do
during the day in between my doctors' appointments. I
spent a good amount of time every day in front of the
computer and on the phone with insurance companies
and provider offices. We had to create a spreadsheet with
multiple worksheets attached just to track medical billing
and record who the provider was, the date of the service,

the service performed, the cost of the service, how much was applied to our deductible, how much was being written off (if it was in-network), how much was covered by insurance, and what our responsibility was for the remaining balance. I entered every piece of mail we received into the spreadsheet and then color-coded what was outstanding with insurance, what was paid in full, whether or not it applied toward our deductible, whether or not it was a duplicate bill, and a running total of how much we owed. It was a very detailed, elaborate spreadsheet.

Another piece of good news was that Jon and I had very good insurance and a savings account. God really provided for us financially—if we didn't have either of those items, we would have had to file for bankruptcy! Insurance covered 90 percent of our medical bills, but when you are talking hundreds of thousands of dollars' worth of expenses, there is still a lot to pay out of pocket. It seemed like every day I would call and talk with a provider's office to put together payment plans. I took notes regarding who I spoke with and what we discussed. I would write notes in the spreadsheet and on the invoices and then file them away in the filing cabinet specifically designated for my accident. All this at age twenty-one.

* * *

A few months had passed since my accident occurred. I was approaching a couple significant turning points in my recovery. First, I would be able to start putting weight on my right leg and relearn how to walk. Also, the rupture in my intestines had healed, so I was able to schedule surgery to have my colostomy reversed. I had survived the winter, using crutches in the snow and ice, and had gotten along fairly well with the colostomy bag, but I was ready to put both of those things behind me. On the night before I was cleared to put weight on my right leg, I took my first steps.

To say I was anxiously awaiting this moment would be an understatement. I started on my side of the bed and walked around to Jon's side holding onto the frame with one hand. My leg was very weak, and it was just barely strong enough to bear my weight, but I was giddy to be able to stand on both legs. I kept squealing over and over, "Look Jon! I'm walking!"

In that moment, I was joyful, but a few nights later I had the strangest dream. I was back in the same living room where, as a child, my dad sat me on his lap and told me he was diagnosed with ALS. In the dream, my dad told me that I would have children, and the most import-ant thing in my life was to raise them to know the Lord. *What?!*

The dream left me so confused. Here I was, hardly able to walk. Having children was the furthest thing from my mind because I couldn't even mentally process putting one foot in front of the other. How could I get pregnant, carry a baby, and *become a mom?* I knew the dream was from God, though, so I did my best to receive it in faith. I was excited not only to have seen my dad and hear him talk again, but also to have him encourage me to let go of any worry I would have surrounding children. The dream gave me underlying hope for my future as I focused on the difficult task at hand, relearning how to walk.

Yes, I was able to take a couple of steps and hobble around, but walking was going to be very different for me now. Because I didn't have feeling in my foot, I couldn't always tell when I was touching the ground. I could kick my leg out to take a step, but as I tried to pull my leg through for the next step, I had to use momentum to swing it around. In addition, I had drop foot, which meant I was unable to lift the front part of my foot. To walk, I had to hike my hip up to give enough clearance for my foot. I knew I would have a very bad limp for a while, and relearning to walk was going to be a long journey.

Because my pelvis fracture was now healed, I could increase the amount of exercises I was allowed to do at physical therapy. Part of me couldn't help but want to go back to using crutches full time, though. I had gotten so used to the crutches that I could move from point A to point B very quickly. I was much slower on my own two feet. Plus, with crutches, I appeared to be recovering from an injury. Without crutches, I looked severely disabled.

Since walking wasn't panning out quite as well as I had hoped and more complicated than I had imagined, doctors made me a custom drop-foot brace that could help me with my gait. It covered the bottom of my foot and had hinges at the ankle that would spring back up when I took a step. Two metal bars ran parallel up my leg, and the brace strapped just below my knee. Obviously, I couldn't wear any of the shoes I owned. I had to buy all new shoes, and being a typical woman, I was disappointed that I couldn't wear any of my favorite styles. No flip flops, heels, or any type of attractive feminine shoe—only large, ugly orthopedic shoes. The brace also made my right leg longer than my left, and the springs randomly squeaked when I walked. Finally, because of the lack of feeling, I didn't know if my toes were straight in the brace or if I was rubbing an ulcer. I had to be careful every time I put it on. I hid the brace with long pants in the winter, but I was still extremely self-conscious about it and dreaded having to wear it in the summer. I hated the way it looked, but I couldn't walk if I didn't wear it.

That stupid brace was another thing God used to teach me. I'd never realized how much of my pride and self-worth had been tied to my athletic ability. I began to have a bit of an identity crisis as I felt more and more like

Confusion

I was in someone else's body. *Who is this stranger who can't walk without causing a scene?!* Without realizing it, prior to my accident, I had been relying on my flesh and not fully relying on God. When my body failed me, I didn't know who I had become. Now that I was on the road to recovery, I was searching to find meaning and a new purpose for myself. *If the gifts God gave me have been stripped away, is there anything good in me left to offer?* I wondered. It was in those reflections where God brought Galatians 2:20 to my mind: "I have been crucified with Christ and I no longer live, but Christ lives in me. The life I now live in the body, I live by faith in the Son of God, who loved me and gave himself for me." Slowly but surely, I began to shift my confidence and hope off myself and back onto Christ. It was a process, but God was faithful and patient.

Physical therapy went from performing exercises on a table to walking in a straight line, which was harder than it sounds. I had terrible balance. I couldn't tell when I was touching the ground, and my leg was too weak to hold my weight. Therapists would time me standing on one leg to see how long I could hold my balance—even a few seconds was an improvement from one day to the next. As my leg grew stronger, I would add more exercises. Then came the day I started therapy on a treadmill. Unfortunately, it was another slap in the face. The treadmill reminded me of my former life. It was how I trained for races in the past. I would crank it up and run for forty-five minutes to an hour at a time. As I stepped onto the treadmill and turned it on this time, I lost my balance. I couldn't even *stand* on the machine anymore, let alone move on it. I held on to the handle bars as my therapist held on to me, and I walked for one minute. That was it. On to the next exercise. I felt defeated, but there was a little bit of excitement in me knowing that it would get easier from there.

The elliptical machine I knew would be much more promising. It would be easier to build up cardio because I had more points of contact to keep my balance. My feet were enclosed so they couldn't slide off the machine. As soon as I received the clear, I jumped in my car, drove myself over to the community recreation center, put on my headphones, and climbed onto the elliptical. I was so ecstatic that I was able to *work out* again. It gave me hope that I could have some normalcy back in my daily routine. I never thought I would take working out for granted until I didn't have the ability to do what I loved. That day in the gym, I had the best work out I had ever experienced. Even though it was only fifteen minutes long, it was still fifteen minutes of doing something I had doubted would ever be a part of my life again. I was praising God the whole time.

Progress had been made on the orthopedic side of things, but now I needed to address the intestine poking out the side of my stomach. On to the next surgery! We drove to Denver for a few follow-up appointments and to schedule the colostomy reversal. Once we got there, we were told that the doctor who performed my surgery was no longer at that hospital. He was only on rotation at the time of my accident and had moved to another location. Both Jon and I were disappointed, but we assumed there was a reason God didn't want that doctor to perform the surgery. Our families suggested we go back to Kansas for the reversal. The surgery required a long hospital stay, and we honestly could use their help. In addition, a top surgeon in Kansas City who knew our family and had been following my recovery wanted to do the surgery. So, we started the fourteen-hour drive back to Kansas to undergo my fifth surgery in four months.

6.

Setbacks

It was an emotional homecoming. Our parents and a few of our siblings had visited us at St. Anthony's Hospital in Denver, but there was a lot of family I hadn't seen since the accident. We shed tears when I saw my brother for the first time, along with my sisters-in-law, nieces and nephews, grandparents, aunts, uncles, and cousins. I was full of mixed emotions because I was excited to see them, but I also saw how torn up they were knowing what I had been through.

Going home to Kansas was the first time I realized just how much my accident had affected other people. I felt guilty and humbled. I knew all they had for me was love, but I was nervous. I could tell by the looks on everyone's faces that they didn't feel like they were looking at the Kim they once knew. They were happy to see me walking around, but they felt sorry for me too. The last thing I wanted was for anyone to feel sorry for me or treat me any differently than they had in the past. Just like I had been struggling internally with my identity crisis, my family was also going through their own version of figuring out how to relate to my new physical limitations and to me. Everyone wanted to see the scars and hear what happened. They looked at me in astonishment as I walked them through everything that had transpired over the past few months. They read my emotions as I told stories to figure out whether to laugh or cry at the experiences I shared. After spending a couple of days catching up with family and friends, it was back to business. I had to start preparing for my reverse colostomy.

I was so eager for the day to come. I met with the doctor who would be performing the surgery a few days before, and he was gentle and kind. He took the time to cover every detail of the procedure—how long it was expected to take, how many days I would be in the hospital, and when I would be free to travel back to Durango. There were a few things I had to do in preparation, which was going to be the most unpleasant part of the whole experience. I had to "cleanse my system," and I had to do it multiple times. The first round consisted of drinking a bottle of magnesium citrate to prep for a colonoscopy. It tasted terrible, and I still can't drink Sprite to this day. I went through a couple colostomy bags and the next morning headed to the hospital to have the procedure done.

Because the initial surgery to create the colostomy was performed in an emergency situation and we couldn't contact the surgeon who performed it, no one really knew what the doctors would be getting into when they opened me this time. The purpose of the pre-op colonoscopy would be to confirm that the perforated area of my colon was indeed healed and that I had enough healthy intestines left to reattach everything.

When I woke up, the report had come back that everything looked healthy, so I was cleared to proceed with the surgery. I went back to my mom's house to start the second round of prep for the surgery, and this time, instead of just drinking a bottle of magnesium citrate, I had to take a laxative tablet once every fifteen minutes and drink an exorbitant amount of Gatorade. Meanwhile, everyone around me at the dinner table that evening was enjoying steak and potatoes.

It was a short drive to the hospital the next morning, and I was able to check in for the first time without going through the emergency room. The room was calm, the nurses were relaxed, and I was able to take my time changing out of my clothes and into the hospital gown. As soon as I was ready, the medical team came in to roll me back to the operating room. I kissed my mom and Jon goodbye and even bid my "Stinky Stoma" farewell.

Once I arrived in the operating room I was asked to crawl up onto the metal operating table—I felt like I was crawling onto an altar to be sacrificed! The table was cold, and there were bright lights everywhere. It felt unintuitive to lie down of my own free will, but I trusted that the doctors knew what they were doing. I prayed as they put an oxygen mask on me, and the next thing I knew, I was waking up from surgery.

You have no concept of time when you are under anesthesia. A thirty-minute procedure feels the same as a six-hour surgery, which is how long my procedure ended up taking. When I woke up, my family was surrounding my bed and looking a bit frazzled, stressed, and tired. I had no idea why they all looked so concerned. It turns out that my three-hour surgery had turned into six-hours because of the amount of scar tissue I had in my abdomen. When I had my colonoscopy, the inside of my intestines looked great, but there were still unknowns regarding the condition of my abdomen until they made the incision and actually looked at it.

God had a very specific reason why he didn't want my operation to take place in Denver. He wanted *this* surgeon to perform the surgery. He knew *this* surgeon would take the time necessary to remove all the scar tissue and put my internal organs back in place. We learned that because I hit the tree at such a rapid rate, my internal organs were jarred out of their natural position. Not only did the surgeon reattach my intestines (reverse my colostomy), but he also cleaned out all the scar tissue that had built up from the trauma my body had been through. He put my uterus and fallopian tubes back where they belonged and removed cysts from my ovaries. He also removed my appendix and finished the surgery by placing a material around my abdomen to keep the scar tissue from growing back, or at least keep it to a minimum.

I will be forever grateful for the surgeon who performed my surgery that day. I knew I had received special treatment, and the fact that he cared enough to make sure my uterus, fallopian tubes, and ovaries were where they should be gave me that much more of a chance to have children someday. This time, when I lifted my hospital gown after the surgery to look at my stomach, the colostomy bag was gone, and there were just a few stitches to show where it once was. I had stitches down my stomach creating a large scar, but the stitches didn't look as intimidating as the staples had. I praised God that the surgery went well and I no longer had to live with a colostomy bag. Now all I had to do was stay in the hospital and wait for my intestines to start moving again.

When you undergo intestinal surgery of any kind, your intestines essentially freeze. Usually, they are constantly contracting, digesting, and processing the food you eat, but when you interfere with that cycle, they stop functioning normally. It takes a few days for them to start contracting again. In order for the surgeon to monitor my progress and see if the reversal was successful, I had to stay in the hospital until my intestines started to function. Doctors told me that it typically takes around seven days for them to start moving again, but they also told me that because my surgery took twice as long, it may take longer.

I shared my hospital room with a roommate, which was slightly uncomfortable and humbling, to say the least, because there was only a thin curtain separating my bedside commode and me from a stranger who was in the same amount of discomfort. The nursing staff slowly started adding food back into my diet to trigger contractions, but when they listened to my stomach with a stethoscope, they couldn't detect any movement. After about the fifth day, I was starting to become restless. The nurses would come get me out of bed every couple of hours to go for a "walk" around the hospital to try to trigger a reaction. They also started reducing my pain medicine (even though I was still in pain) to make the laxatives more effective. Though I was hoping to be out of the hospital prior to Easter, Easter came and went, and so did my roommate. In fact, several roommates came and went. Every couple of days, one roommate was released, and another one was brought in.

I had to throw more and more vanity out the window.

As the nurses would try to increase my diet, it made me sick. The food would go down, and shortly after that, it would come back up. I started to go stir crazy. Every once in a while, I'd be able to get out and enjoy nice weather or time with Jon, but I couldn't help but overall feel disheartened as I continued to wait.

Since I was already in the hospital and simply buying time, the doctors ordered another EMG on my leg to check the status of my nerve damage. We would compare these results to the original test taken just a couple of days after my initial accident. I had been praying that God would heal me completely, and I truly believed that's what he wanted. The problem was, my expectations were for him to heal me instantaneously. After all, that was what I wanted. When the results came back and the neurologist gave me the news, I was crushed. The results were not much different from the ones I'd received after my first EMG in the emergency room months before. The nerves in my upper leg were still damaged. The doctor did think there was a slight chance I would get some additional mobility back, but he highly doubted I would ever recover any use of my lower leg.

I shouldn't have been shocked by my results, but I interpreted them as, "God isn't answering my prayers." It struck a nerve. I broke down in tears. I don't mean a few tears—I mean inconsolable, body-shaking, hyperventilating, waterfall tears. I knew I shouldn't have expected anything different, but I had built up expectations in my head without even knowing it. I really thought the results would be better or different in some way, but when that didn't happen, I thought God didn't care, or I was doing something wrong. It didn't even occur to me that God had wanted this journey to be a marathon, not a sprint.

So there I was—it was the day doctors and nurses told me my intestines would start moving again, and they weren't. And now I was being reminded that, yes, I did still have nerve damage in my right leg, and there wasn't much of a chance for recovery. To say I was disappointed and angry would be an understatement. I wasn't worried about my survival at this point; I was worried about the long-term effects.

The eighth day passed, as well as the ninth, and still no movement. Talk of going back to a colostomy bag began circulating, which was the absolute last thing I wanted. I did everything in my power to make things speed up, but I was getting weak by this point because I hadn't been able to keep food down. The nurses started giving me calories through my IV to keep my weight from dropping too quickly, and then finally, out of the blue, at the two-week mark, my intestines started functioning. Praise God—*finally*! I could digest food without a colostomy. The medical staff was just as relieved as I was to sign the discharge papers.

I was glad to be out of the hospital, but physically, I felt horrible. I hadn't really eaten anything for two weeks. I had lost a lot of weight, and the idea of eating made me nauseous. I had no appetite. I knew I needed calories, but nothing sounded good. My mom scrambled some eggs one morning, and I choked them down. After I finished eating, I went to sit outside in the grass. It was springtime, and the weather was beautiful. My sister-in-law and niece had come by for a visit, and we sat and watched as my niece ran around and played.

You'd think that since I had been released from the hospital, I would be on Cloud Nine, but my attitude started to spiral downward rapidly as reality started to settle in again. I had been trying to see my situation through God's eyes and believe he had a good plan for my life, but it was hard not to focus on the moment and how I felt *in* that moment. Amidst what should have been joy, everything seemed so big and insurmountable. Yes, it was a beautiful day. Yes, I was able to sit in the grass and soak up the sun. And yes, I was finally out of the hospital, which I had been praying for. I was with family at my mom's house, and I was able to eat. God had answered so many prayers. But emotionally I was hitting rock bottom. I felt like I was on the outside, looking in at my life, and I could barely move as I mindlessly watched my niece running around. Fear started to creep in again:

Great. The surgeon fixed my uterus, fallopian tubes, and ovaries, but I will never have the energy or ability to keep up with a toddler. I can't be a mom. I can barely walk, and my balance is horrible. How will I ever be able to safely carry my own baby around? Can my body withstand a pregnancy? My children will be ashamed and embarrassed of me! What does my niece think of me? Everyone used to compare her to me with her energy and athletic ability. Now she won't even want to be associated with me . . .

This time, I wasn't able to muster the faith I once had. I hurried inside to the bedroom, shut the door, threw myself on the bed, and started to cry.

To make matters worse, Jon had to go back to work in Durango. His employer had been more than accommodating with time off, but Jon didn't want to take advantage of his generosity. Plus, we knew we had more medical bills headed our way. Jon needed to fly home, but I was in no condition to travel. The plan was for me to join him in Durango once I had gained more strength and worked back to a normal diet. I cried as Jon left, not knowing exactly when I would see him again. I was surrounded by family, but felt alone.

Setbacks

This was common throughout my experience of healing. I tried to keep a good attitude and positive outlook,
but sometimes I failed. I often entered periods of depres-
sion. Some days I would be like Peter and walk on water,
eyes fixed on the Lord. The storm would swirl around me,
but I was able to withstand it. I trusted. I had faith. But
other days, I would look to the storm. Fixated on circumstances alone, I began to sink. It would only be a matter
of time before I drowned.

I am grateful to the Lord for seeing me through these
highs and lows. If there was anything constant in my journey of healing, it was his assurance that though I often felt
defeated, he wasn't finished with me yet. "For I am confident of this very thing," Paul assures us in Philippians.
"He who began a good work in you will perfect it until the
day of Christ Jesus" (Philippians 1:6, NASB).

7.

Progress

The weather was starting to warm up outside, so it was time to deal with the moment I had been dreading: wearing shorts. At this point, my leg was completely atrophied, and my fear of people staring at me proved legitimate as I walked around with a squeaky brace. My mom knew how much this bothered me, and she wanted to cheer me up, so she took me shopping to find shoes that were more feminine, but still functional. She also bought me a new wardrobe because I had dropped three sizes and couldn't keep my pants up. Having spruced up my appearance gave me more confidence to go out in public, but it was still painful to see heads turn and stare as people tried to figure out what my injuries were. Or worse, sometimes I would run into friends who hadn't heard the news of my accident, and I was unrecognizable to them.

It had been over a month since my colostomy reversal, and I started to become concerned. My appetite had increased, so food was going in, but nothing had come out since I left the hospital. I began to suffer pretty intense cramping, so I scheduled an appointment with my surgeon to find out if this was normal, or if we needed to be concerned. He suggested I add fiber to my diet and increase my stool softener. All this did was make me very sick, though. The fiber expanded in my stomach and made me nauseous, and the cramping intensified. With each cramp the pain increased and eventually landed me back in the emergency room.

Something was very wrong, so the doctors ordered a CT scan immediately. I choked down another bottle of the chalky white formula, but that was enough to put me over the edge. My belly became so bloated I looked like I was nine months pregnant! I started vomiting uncontrollably and was in a tailspin; it felt like my intestines were going to explode. *I thought the pain associated with the broken pelvis was bad,* I remember thinking. *This is way worse!*

I started to fade. I don't know where the nurses took me, but the room turned all white and began spinning so much I couldn't keep my eyes open. My mom was terrified and didn't know what to do. She had seen me at my worst in ICU, but this was the most sick I'd ever been. I was in and out of consciousness, but I remember thinking, *Why would God have me go through so many surgeries and endure so much pain for me to die now?* Logically, nothing made any sense. I didn't think I was going to make it, and at this point, I didn't know if I even *wanted* to.

My mom called my brother, who lived an hour away, to come be with us at the hospital. She told him she didn't think I was going to survive, and she needed his support. The next phone call was to Jon in Durango. She tried to get me to talk to him, but I couldn't—I was moaning and in too much pain. Jon immediately booked the next flight out of Durango to be with me. The thought of knowing he was on his way made me want to stay alive. I don't remember anything else about that night, but when I woke up in the hospital the next day, Jon was there next to me.

The results of the CT scan were inconclusive, but I was admitted to the hospital and knew I wasn't going anywhere until we found the root of the problem. Surgery was risky because my bowels were full; if they perforated, it would result in another e-coli infection. The doctors needed to find out what was causing the obstruction, though. A colonoscopy was less risky but could still result in surgery. I had to sign a release form that stated I acknowledged the risk and also consented to having emergency surgery for another colostomy if things went wrong. I, of course, didn't want another colostomy, but at this point, I felt so horrible I didn't care what happened. I just wanted out of pain. I signed the form, and off I went for my second colonoscopy, not knowing where I would wake up.

When I did wake up, I was pleasantly surprised with good news. I did not have to have emergency surgery, and they found the source of the problem. The culprit was scar tissue. Apparently, the area where my intestines were re-connected had almost completely swelled shut. The doctors were able to slowly dilate the tissue and felt confident it would solve the problem long term if they were to do the same procedure a few more times over the course of a month. In the meantime, I was put on a clear liquid—and I mean *clear liquid*—diet and sent home. Whatever I drank I had to be able to hold it up and see straight through it. No milk, no tomato juice, not even Ensure. I could drink Gatorade, bouillon cubes dissolved in hot water, popsicles, and that's about it . . . for a month.

Throughout that month I would go in once a week for a colonoscopy to have my intestines dilated, and every time, I had to sign the same release papers consenting to an emergency surgery should a problem arise. Each visit, I would get worked up and fear the worst. I lost a lot of weight, and I hadn't had a lot to lose. I weighed around 125 pounds when I was released from the hospital, and after being on my clear liquid diet, I was down to under 105. I weighed myself every morning, and the numbers just kept going down. My skin was pale, I was losing hair, and I wasn't absorbing any nutrition. If I thought I was self-conscious going out in public before, I was even more so now. I looked—and practically was—anorexic. It was scary; I didn't know how much more weight I could stand to lose.

One night, at another one of my breaking points, I found myself lying prostrate on the ground crying out to God and pleading for his help. I knew he created me and could heal me, but I didn't understand why he was taking so long. Nothing was easy. The trial hadn't let up—I felt like I was pressed up against a wall with no options other than to simply wait for healing. The results were out of my control; they were *always* out of my control. I was tired of waiting on God's timing. I had initially planned on being in Kansas City for a month. I had now been there for two months and expected to stay for at least three. "Humble yourselves, therefore, under God's mighty hand . . . "The words of 1 Peter are so clear to me now, but I couldn't hear them then. I had thrown myself before him, and now I know he heard my cries. "Cast all your anxiety on Him because He cares for you" (1 Peter 5:6-7).

* * *

Another surgery deadline was quickly approaching. Doctors recommended that the plate and screws be removed from my pelvis after six months to reduce the chance of infection. Believe it or not, I was actually looking forward to the hardware removal because the screws had become uncomfortable. Still, I wasn't sure I was actually going to be able to *have* the surgery. It had been on the schedule for a few months, but at this point, the date didn't seem realistic because I still wasn't eating solid foods. I kept the surgery date and found the faith to trust that God would heal me in time to undergo the operation.

I had time on my hands, so I needed to occupy my mind. I was still determined to finish my degree, so I decided to enroll in an online course to help chip away at some of my credit hours. I took a financial management class and received an A in the course. Finally my confidence started to build that there was a life outside of the hospital. I could look forward to things other than surgeries! I became thankful all over again that I didn't suffer head trauma at the time of my accident and praised God that I had the ability to study. I could still earn my degree and have a career. I had a renewed determination to keep persevering.

After my fifth and final colonoscopy, my doctor told me that my intestines had progressed enough for me to start adding soft food back into my diet. I could now eat tomato soup, scrambled eggs, oatmeal, and bananas. I went straight back to my mom's house and had two bowls of tomato soup. It hit the spot . . . I didn't even realize I *liked* tomato soup!

Things were finally moving in the right direction again. I was two weeks away from my scheduled surgery, and out of nowhere, my intestines started functioning completely normally again, without causing me any pain. Praise God! I started increasing my diet, which obviously made me feel 100% better because I was finally receiving some nutrition and gaining strength. I was ready to pack up and head to Denver for my sixth surgery. Jon and I kissed family goodbye and headed to Denver to remove the hardware.

* * *

Doctors told me this would not be an invasive surgery, but I still wasn't looking forward to having my pelvis incision cut back open for the fifth time. The procedure didn't take long, though, and I only had to stay in the hospital one night. I ran into a few nurses who cared for me during my initial stay, and I was happy to report back to them that I no longer had a colostomy bag. I also took the opportunity to thank them for everything they had done to bring me back to health.

Now that the plate and screws were out of my body, the doctor approved the removal of the PICC line and put me on oral antibiotics. Finally, all the attachments were gone—the bag hanging from my stomach, all the drains, the plate and screws that had been rubbing under my skin, and the PICC line. The surgery was the last immediate one on the agenda, so I knew that I could finally take a break from hospitals and try to get back to somewhat of a normal lifestyle. I would eventually need knee surgery, but I could schedule that down the road.

For the first time in months, my health wasn't dictating my every move. Jon and I were thrilled to finally be able to head home to Durango together. The first thing I did when we arrived was enroll in classes for the fall semester. It was now the middle of July; I would start back to college in exactly one month.

8.

New Normal

Overall, my reverse colostomy was successful, but I still ran into problems from time to time. The doctors had stretched the area where they reattached my intestines as far as they felt comfortable dilating it. They were afraid if they stretched any further, they may compromise the tissue and cause the intestines to perforate again. Their hope was that over time, my body would absorb any additional scar tissue and naturally correct itself.

That did eventually happen, but it was over a two-year period. And during that two-year period, I would find myself in the emergency room at least once a month or once every two months with extreme abdominal pain. I could almost track, to the day, when it would happen, and I knew there was nothing I could do to prevent it. I tried everything. I would start drinking bottles of magnesium citrate a couple days before I thought the cramping would start, but that never resulted in anything. I would switch to a liquid diet, but inevitably around 9:30-10:00 at night, my stomach would start cramping as I was getting ready for bed. I would start vomiting and then black out, and Jon would rush me to the emergency room. My poor husband saw me get sick more times than anyone ever deserves. He saw me sick more often than healthy. Going to the hospital became such a routine that we had it down and understood exactly what needed to be done. I knew Jon needed to go to work the next day, and if he stayed in the hospital with me all night, he would be too tired to work. So our routine was that he would help check me into the emergency room, kiss me good night, and head home. I would then stay there as they ran the same tests they always did and come to the same conclusion—that I was impacted.

In the midst of all this I often wondered, *Is this going to go on for the rest of my life, God? What did I do to deserve this chronic pain? I know you can heal me completely! Why are you allowing me to suffer?* I continued to pray and journal daily that God would heal my intestines. After all, I knew he saw my pain: "Record my misery; list my tears on your scroll—are they not in your record?" (Psalm 56:8).

Over time, the back-and-forth of my new routine started to wear on me, so much so that I began to hide my feelings from those around me. I was tired of talking to people about my health all the time. I knew that the only reason friends and family, even strangers, asked me about my recovery was because they genuinely loved and cared for me and wanted to offer their assistance and their prayers, but I was fed up. I downplayed how I felt most of the time. If people asked me how I was doing, I would put a smile on and tell them I was doing great. I would even hide details of hospital stays from friends and family because they happened so regularly. I was tired of being the center of attention, or worse, a burden. There were times I went to the hospital, and my family never even found out. Jon would drop me off at night, and I would call him later that afternoon when I was cleared to leave to have him pick me up. And then, like clockwork, the next day, I would shower, put on make-up, do my hair, dress, and head to class. No one ever knew what had happened the night before.

The good news amidst frequent tests and hospital visits was that for the first time in nine months, I at least didn't have a pressing surgery schedule. By this time, I had enrolled as a full-time student, and in-between classes I would attend physical therapy. I had been doing home exercises and using the e-stim machine the whole time I was in Kansas, but now I was being pushed and advised by my therapists again. I knew they would help me continue to gain strength. My muscles were at their weakest point, but

I was confidant things would only get better.

It was in these early stages of positive progress when part of me unexpectedly began to feel guilty. Yes, I had been in a horrible accident, but God was allowing me to recover. What about all those people who didn't recover—who *wouldn't* recover? Images of my dad when he was sick came to my mind. His ALS was terminal. My dad knew that with each passing day, he would only get weaker, not stronger. My reflections reminded me that I needed to be thankful that I was able to build strength. I needed to remember that positive progress was a good thing to always be grateful for. Suddenly, knowing I could get better began to motivate me in new ways. I started to give everything I had at each physical therapy appointment. I became more disciplined to exercise in my free time. Almost as a way of honoring my dad, I wanted to maximize my recovery potential. I knew I had been given a gift, and I didn't want to waste it.

Since I had encountered my fair share of speed bumps along the academic road, it felt so refreshing to be back in school and into a normal routine. I was already an unconventional student being married, but I was even more so now because of my accident. I took school very seriously. I looked forward to class, was anxious to learn, enjoyed studying, and realized the value of the tuition I was paying. I also enjoyed being around the other students. Could

I totally relate to them? No. I was living a completely different lifestyle. I felt like I had crunched ten years of life experience into the past nine months and was coming back to school a different person. But my friends respected what I had been through and were always there to lend a helping hand if I needed it.

I had additional motivation in school because if I could manage my work load, I would be in a position to graduate the following spring semester. I was determined to earn my degree since I had taken one semester off following our wedding, a second semester off because I fell short of in-state tuition, and a third semester off because of my accident. There was nothing stopping me this time around.

Outside of class and physical therapy, I added going to the community recreation center to my schedule. The stationary bike was now a part of my physical therapy routine, which I loved. One evening after work, Jon decided to join me in the gym. We sat on stationary bikes right next to each other and peddled for about an hour—it was amazing! Jon and I shared the love of exercise. The phrase "those who play together stay together" pretty much defined our relationship. From the instant we started dating up until my accident, we loved pushing ourselves to the max with physical exertion. It didn't matter what the activity was—we were constantly competing with each other, and everyone knew it. Even our wedding gift from Jon's parents was a pair of bikes!

I was, of course, still hesitant to try new things. I found myself extremely self-conscious because I always had to adjust to whatever activity I was attempting. My mind remembered how my body was supposed to respond during specific activities, but I had to change my coordination to make it work with my new limitations. For example, when I rode the stationary bike, I had to use a bike with cages around the pedals. (I could slide my foot into the cage, and it would stay put. Because of my nerve damage, it was impossible for me to ride a bike without them.) I always felt like people were watching me because I had to use my hands to position my leg. In reality, of course, no one really noticed or cared, but I did. I also feared failure and injury. I was worried that I would become discouraged and give up if I wasn't able to physically do the activity, and I was afraid that I would hurt myself trying. It took a lot of trial and error as I added different activities back into my life. Jon was my security blanket; I needed him with me every time I tried something new. I knew God had handpicked him to be my husband and support me through life, but I didn't discover how perfectly paired we were until I faced these intricate parts of my recovery.

We started making the evening bike rides at the gym part of our normal routine. There was a spin class that took place in a classroom next to where we rode, and Jon convinced me to try it with him. Again, I almost refused because I didn't want to draw attention to myself, but I got over my pride and agreed to go. I loved the class! Because I was on a stationary bike I was able to ride at a pace that was comfortable for me, and the class made me feel "athletic" again and almost part of a team. Over time, the class also significantly increased my strength and the co-ordination in my leg. I even bought new bike shoes, which allowed me to clip into the pedal so that my foot was completely secure. This allowed me to really push myself physically without letting my disability get in the way.

As spin class gave me a newfound confidence to try new things, all of a sudden I realized another purpose God had in my sports growing up. For a while I had felt guilty for "wasting my parent's money" on sports now that I was in-jured. But those sports were not a waste at all. God had directed every part of my life. I had developed coordination through all those sports, and that coordination was quickly becoming my greatest asset. I didn't have to learn how to do something from scratch—I could simply relearn an activity with a few tweaks. "The Lord makes firm the steps of the one who delights in him," the psalmist writes. "Though he may stumble, he will not fall, for the Lord upholds him with his hand" (Psalm 37:23-24). Yes, God was holding me up and empowering me in new and exciting ways. He wasn't going to let anything go to waste.

I finished the fall semester with a 4.0 GPA and celebrated the one-year anniversary of my accident by snowshoe-
ing up to the top of Buttermilk Mountain in Aspen with
Jon. Yes, I moved very slowly up the mountain—it took all
day!—but God was physically healing me throughout the
trek. I relied heavily on the ski poles for balance, and the
spikes on the bottom of my snowshoes created traction,
which allowed my feet to grip as I took steps up. I felt tri-
umphant at the top.

Day by day, God was making me whole again and
growing my appreciation for the gifts he had given me—
the things I had taken for granted before, taken pride in.
I was learning that all I had thought I was entitled to and
the accomplishments I took credit for really had very little
to do with me. In reality, everything, *my entire being*, is cred-
ited to God (Acts 17:28).

That year, heading into Christmastime, I was even
more humbled than I was the previous year. The bank
where I had been working prior to my accident was allowing me to work on a part-time basis. I was one semester
away from graduating. I was gaining strength daily and
able to do things physically that I doubted I would ever
be able to do again. God had provided financially for us
to pay off our medical debt, and I still had my husband
standing by my side after two years of marriage. Of all the

things I was thankful for at the end of that first year, my relationship with God was at the very top. It was stronger than it had ever been. I knew now, more than ever, how real God was and how much control he had over my life. I knew I needed to live in submission, and I had a greater respect for everything he had given me. God had made me so in tune with him that I became extra sensitive to callings he placed on my life. From the time I got up in the morning to the time I went to bed, I was continually aware of his presence. This battle was not mine—it was God's (2 Chronicles 20:15). He was fighting it for me and winning!

* * *

That next spring, I was referred to a surgeon in Texas for an experimental nerve-transfer surgery because I was still suffering from neurological damage. I was now in my final semester of school but felt the surgery was worth the risk because the only real inconvenience would be enduring a straight-leg brace and crutches for a few months. Being back in a brace would limit what I was able to do at physical therapy, which meant I would lose the strength I had worked so hard to gain. My leg would atrophy all over again. I also knew I wouldn't be able to go to the gym to work out in the evenings with Jon for a while. Two steps forward, and one step back. Still, I hoped this surgery would prove successful and be worth the frustration.

With the extra free time I had while recovering, I began to think about what my life was going to look like after I graduated from school. I hadn't really given much thought to what I wanted to do with my degree because I had been so focused on simply graduating. I figured I would cross the bridge of "What's next?" when I got there.

Durango is a very tourist-driven town. As far as professional careers are concerned, they are pretty few and far between. There are a handful of options as a business major, which is what I was; you can work at a bank or an insurance company, open your own business, or sell real estate. A lot of new graduates found themselves working at restaurants or the ski resort to get by until a job in their field opened up.

One day, while considering what opportunities I'd be interested in, I found an advertisement for a real estate internship. If I took it on, I would be able to earn three credit hours toward my degree, which would ensure my graduation that spring. I hadn't ever considered working in real estate, but it seemed to be a popular industry, and I had enough curiosity about it that I decided to interview. I had no idea what I was getting myself into, but the agent actually offered me the internship on the spot!

During the internship, I met a lot of other agents in

the industry and became very interested in the possibilities and opportunities a career in real estate could lead to
down the road. Most of all, I knew it would be fairly flexible, and I could create my own hours, which was something I was concerned about knowing my health was still
so unpredictable. I knew I wouldn't be dependable in an
eight-to-five environment. I had a couple years of physical
therapy ahead of me, and I still needed surgery to repair
all the ligament damage in my knee.

As the semester was winding down, I was given the
clear to remove the brace from my nerve-transfer surgery.
The snow had melted, and I was off crutches and clos-
ing in on my long-anticipated graduation day. One of
my goals for graduation was to be off crutches and strong
enough to walk up the stairs and across the stage to receive my diploma. My family knew how important this
day was to me, so they scheduled a trip to Durango to
be there for graduation. The weather couldn't have been
more beautiful. That morning, as I was putting my cap
and gown on, my mom surprised me with a very special
gift. She had taken the diamond out of the engagement
ring my dad had given her and had it remounted as a
necklace for me to wear as I walked across the stage. I
knew my dad would be extremely proud of my fight to
accomplish my goal, and it made everything even more
special to have something that was his hanging around my

neck to symbolize it.

It took five years, three different schools in three different states, a marriage, and a trauma accident, but I finally graduated summa cum laude with a business degree.

9.

Miracles

After graduation, God gave me the confidence to pursue real estate full time. I had enrolled in night classes at a local real estate college to prepare for my state and national licensing exams, and to my surprise, Jon started to take an interest in my newly chosen career path too. He decided to take the classes with me to learn more about the industry. We both figured it was better to be able to spend time together in class in the evenings than to not be able to see each other at all.

The more Jon and I learned about selling and investing in real estate, the more we loved the industry. Durango presented an opportunity to participate in the market at whatever capacity agents wanted to undertake. We really enjoyed learning and growing together and started playing around with the idea of working as a team. This would mean that Jon would have to quit his salaried job

as an engineer, and we would work as independent con-
tractors on a full-commission basis, but we had built our
savings back up and felt like this was the direction God
was calling us to move in. We knew that because God had
given us confidence, he would provide what we needed financially regardless of whether we were working salaried
or commissioned jobs.

It was amazing how God provided for us financially
through my accident and into this new season in our careers. Looking back, I can't help but recall Scriptures that
promise God's provision amidst uncertain times: "And my
God will supply every need of yours according to his rich-
es in glory in Christ Jesus" (Philippians 4:19, NASB). To
this day, we don't know how we managed to pay all our
bills, but when they were due, somehow, we always had
enough money in our checking account to cover them.
Our new venture into real estate was another step of faith
that God was calling us to take, and we needed to look to
him to continue to be our provider. What better way was
there to trust and see God's provision than for us to both
be working a full-commission job?

My confidence was building. We both enjoyed working
hard during the week and playing hard on the weekend.
During that summer, we spent our weekends relearning
activities we had enjoyed together prior to my accident.
A lot of trial and error went into everything we tried. I

was still too unsure of myself to attempt anything for the first time with a group of friends. I wouldn't go hiking or do anything with anyone else unless I felt 100% comfortable and confident doing it with Jon first. God really used this time as a team-building exercise for our marriage. Jon was the only person who had seen every aspect of what I had been through emotionally and physically, and when I failed at something, I knew he wouldn't judge me or think any differently of me. He had the patience of a saint, which allowed me to fall down, pick myself up, and try again. I had to figure out my physical limitations and make adaptations to my shoes, supportive braces, and poles for balance. The goals I set for myself were measurable, which kept me motivated to continue to challenge myself. Because I was starting at the bottom, the only place I could go was up. So even if my progress was limited, it was still progress, and it was enough to get me out of bed the next day and try again.

Working out in a gym was safe, but I wanted to move my activities outside. Since I have a natural love of the outdoors, being outside in God's creation was much more appealing to me than being in a gym. It would be more challenging because the hiking trails in Colorado are not flat, but they do have incentives along the way. "If I hike just ten more minutes," I would tell myself, "there is a breathtaking view of the valley with the river winding through it." Or, "If I make it up this hill, I can see the snow-covered peaks." The first few times I hiked with Jon, he basically carried me up the trail because of my nerve damage. I would trip over rocks and tree roots, I couldn't take a step uphill because my hamstring and glut weren't strong enough yet, and a hiking trail that the majority of people would have no problem climbing, I found myself crawling on all fours to get from point A to point B. I didn't care, though, because I was so excited just to be doing it. Being outside with the sun beating down, the wind blowing, the smell of the pine trees, and the earth below me, I felt so grateful I was able to even *crawl* in the mountains and be surrounded by God.

Hiking turned out to be the best thing for my leg because the more I hiked a trail, the better I knew it. And each time I hiked, I was forced to strengthen the weakest part of my body by challenging it to go uphill. It forced my hamstring and glut to fire and contract, and each day they did, I became stronger.

I can't tell you how many times after my initial accident I thought to myself, *I will never be able to do that again,* and then, how many times God would shock me—and I would shock myself—by being able to accomplish the unimaginable. Ephesians 3:20 was becoming my life verse: "Now to Him who is able to do far more abundantly beyond all that we ask or think, according to the power that works within us, to him be glory in the church and in Christ Jesus throughout all generations, for ever and ever" (NASB). At first after my accident, I had, in a sense, mourned and laid to rest things I *knew* I would "never do again." I had lowered my expectations so much, but as I later finally started to push the boundaries during my recovery, bitterness would turn to joy and praise. My confidence would grow slowly, slowly . . . and then there was a snowball effect.

Once my confidence grew with hiking, I decided to figure out how to ride my bike again. Again, Jon had talked me into riding a stationary bike and even gave me the courage to attend spin classes, but riding a bike outside was a whole other challenge. Yes, I was using clips on the stationary bike because my right foot was paralyzed, but I didn't have to worry about balance or what would happen if I tried to clip out when I was done riding. Jon encouraged me to try riding a regular bike. We headed over to a field across from our house so that when I fell, I at least had somewhat of a soft landing. We set the clips on the pedals to their loosest setting, still allowing me to clip my right foot in so it was secure. Then, like a parent teaching a child to ride a bike, Jon had a hold of the seat and started to push me so I could pedal. I was able to use the momentum I created by pushing down on my left side to keep the wheels turning, which allowed me to mimic the motion on the right side. I couldn't believe it! I was riding an actual bike on my own!

I was doing great while I kept the movement going, but I hadn't quite figured out the dismount yet. I ended up riding toward Jon, putting on my breaks, and letting him catch me. We then practiced starting and stopping. I quickly figured out that the only way for me to get off the bike was to unclip my left foot and dismount that way. If for whatever reason I lost my balance and had to fall to the right, I was just going to go down with the bike because I couldn't physically unclip that foot. And even if I was able to unclip without using my hands, my leg wasn't strong enough to hold my weight up. Falling down was a risk I was willing to take.

At that point, the possibilities were endless because riding a bike was something I had put on my "will never do again" list. The fact that I was doing it breathed life into all the other things still on that list. I slowly went from riding in a field, to riding on the river trail, to riding fifty miles on a road bike. I even built the confidence up to try mountain-biking trails, which to me was the ultimate accomplishment because mountain biking challenges your balance more than any other type of riding. It also took more coordination for me as I had less control regarding how I clipped in and out of my bike. My riding wasn't pretty all the time; I fell a lot and would get really frustrated, even hurt, at times. (One time I fell right on top of a cactus.) It took practice, over and over again, to retrain my body how to react and respond. The training my body went through, though, developed strength, balance, and coordination that I could transfer back to my everyday life, improving my ability to walk.

Nothing I ever did to recover was without consequences. The more I exercised, the worse my nerve pain was in the evening, the more I would have stomach cramping, and the more likely I was to develop blisters or ulcers on my foot because my shoes or braces were bound to rub on areas I couldn't feel as I was exerting energy. But all those things paled in comparison to the fact that exercising was making me stronger and allowing my body to heal beyond what anyone thought was possible. It allowed me to heal both emotionally and physically. The benefits outweighed the risks. I was seeing so many improvements on a daily basis that I couldn't keep from wanting to try more. I eventually got to a point where I was stronger on a bike than I was before my accident. Jon and I started joking that I could ride for miles on a bike, but as soon as I got off it, I couldn't walk without assistance.

Days turned into weeks, weeks turned into months, and months turned into years. My nerves were slowly regenerating, and my muscles continued to get stronger. I successfully figured out how to downhill ski again, learned how to skate ski for the first time, and spent summers hiking mountains. God was slowly healing me over time, but the one injury that wasn't making any progress was my drop foot. The experimental nerve-transfer surgery in Houston hadn't been successful. I even flew to Denver to have a tendon transfer performed on my ankle, which provided a little more stability, but it didn't fix the problem. I was so confused because every time I started journaling, I heard God tell me that he would heal me completely. I went around and around with him on this and shed tons of tears. Each disappointment took me right back to the emotional place I found myself in as a sixteen-year-old girl when God didn't spare my dad's life. He didn't heal my father.

The more I reflected on my experiences, the more I realized that my dad's death and my accident made me question my faith, or at best, put God in a box of things he "can do" and "can't do." He had proven himself completely faithful and performed so many miracles in my life, but I *still* struggled with my belief that God would follow through on something he was telling me. I had developed very subtle insensitivity as God took his time teaching me lessons and growing my faith. "And without faith it is impossible to please God," I kept telling myself, "because anyone who comes to him must believe that he exists and that he rewards those who earnestly seek him" (Hebrews

11:6). Each day that I took steps forward and backward in my recovery, I also took steps forward and backward in my faith.

More time passed, and the scar tissue in my abdomen had started to reabsorb and wasn't causing reoccurring pain. My pelvis also was healed, the nerves in my upper leg regenerated, and my knee was operational. I knew I still needed surgery to repair the damaged ligaments and torn meniscus, but they could be fixed. The nerve damage in my foot, though, was becoming unbearable. I constantly had ulcers on my foot that I managed on a daily basis. I was warned by podiatrists to keep an eye on them to make sure they didn't get infected, but I didn't think in comparison to everything else I had been through that a "blister" was a big deal. Over time, though, one of the ulcers spiraled out of control. I had accidently dislocated my toe, and the bone was poking through the blister on the bottom of my foot. One day, I looked down and saw the damage. I had been managing what I believed to be a blister on the bottom of my toe for months, but I hadn't taken the time to really *look* at the bottom of my foot. As soon as I realized the extent of the damage, I immediately made an appointment to see a doctor. The doctor saw the injury, cultured it, and scheduled immediate surgery to amputate my toe because it had turned into a staph infection.

The thought of having something amputated bothered me spiritually much more than the previous surgeries I had gone through. How would I ever be healed completely if someone cuts off my toe? I battled with this and was distraught. I was questioning my faith and doubting everything I had ever heard God tell me. If I mistook being told that God would heal me, what other convictions and words God gave me were false? I contacted my mentor and cried to her about these very real fears. She told me that she and her husband wanted to come by our house the night before my surgery to pray over my toe. I know—ridiculous. A toe? Of all the other major injuries I had been dealing with up until this point, a toe was pretty minor. But spiritually, my confidence in God was riding on it, which crushed my spirit more than anything else.

Our friends came over and prayed with Jon and me in our living room and—no joke—after they left, before I headed to bed, I looked at the bottom of my foot, and the gaping hole where my bone was sticking out had a thin layer of skin that had formed to seal it off. It was an ulcer that had been open for months, without any sign of healing. My toe didn't look normal, but skin doesn't grow over an infection like that in a thirty-minute period. I couldn't believe my eyes. When I went into my doctor's office the following morning to prep for surgery, he took one look, and the same disbelief I had the night before was showing all over his face. He was amazed—my toe was healing on its own. My doctor told me that I had some kind of healing power, to which I said we had prayed for God to heal it the night before, and he heard our prayers. God healed my toe by ridding it of infection. The doctor told me he didn't see any need to amputate, but he still wanted to operate and put a rod in the bone to correct the dislocation and fix the ligaments. I didn't care what he did—as long as he didn't cut off my toe!

Right then and there, God showed me that he does, in fact, have the ability to heal instantaneously. You hear of people being healed, but it didn't happen for my dad and, up until that point, it hadn't happened for me. But God showed me that he absolutely, without a doubt, can heal. His healing is simply according to his will and his timing for his purposes. God used something as insignificant as a toe to show me that he was in complete control. I learned that he is not as concerned with our physical well-being as he is with our spiritual well-being. I'm honestly not sure, had I not attached so much *spiritual* meaning to a mere toe, that God would have healed it. He had been slowly healing my body all along, and growing my faith through the process, but none of it had boosted my faith and confidence as much as seeing him graciously heal my toe.

I have been tempted in my life to believe that maybe it's best not to have faith that God will answer my prayers so that I can protect his reputation. *I'd hate to come right out and say that I trust God to heal me completely, and then he proves himself to be unworthy of that trust.* Sound familiar? What I've learned, though, is that faith always involves risk. If we do not have a risk of failure, we do not have genuine faith. God reminds us over and over again in his Word that he loves it when we place our hope in him. Over and over again, God asks us to believe in him, put our faith in him, and "trust in the Lord with all your heart and lean not on your own understanding" (Proverbs 3:5).

Throughout my accident, recovery, and healing journey, God continually met me where I was. It took years, but God has slowly restored me. If he had healed me instantaneously, I would not have drawn so close to him and deepened my walk and relationship with him. My healing would not have left such a big impression on my life and been such a huge testament to others. What I have learned is that *because* my healing took time, I have no choice but to give all credit to God; I can't deny his provision in my life.

God was testing me and teaching me what faith really means: "Now faith is confidence in what we hope for and assurance about what we do not see" (Hebrews 11:1). The more I placed my faith in him to guide my life, the deeper my faith became and the more powerful the gift. God says he freely gives all things: "He who did not spare his own Son, but gave him up for us all—how will he not also, along with him, graciously give us all things?" (Romans 8:32). God gave me the gift of faith and then used it to sustain me.

* * *

It had now been four years since my accident occurred, but I still hadn't addressed my knee injury. I had put surgery off as long as possible. The squeaky wheel gets the grease, and up until that point, all my past surgeries had time limitations with regards to emergency status or windows of opportunity for success. And then, after my unsuccessful nerve transfer and tendon transfer, I was in no hurry to have another operation. I needed to take a breather and try to live a "normal" life even if just for a moment. I also knew that the muscles I had worked so hard to strengthen with physical therapy and cycling would atrophy as soon as I went back to a straight-leg brace following knee surgery. It had taken me so long to make progress, and it made me sick to know that it would all go away with another procedure. But at this point, I was active enough and risked *more* damage if I didn't stabilize my knee ligaments.

I had another MRI and met with my orthopedic surgeon for a consultation to find out the details of the operation. My PCL couldn't be repaired as it completely tore during the initial injury; they would have to rebuild it using a cadaver's Achilles tendon. The good news was that my ACL and LCL, which had minor tears, had actually healed over time. My meniscus, on the other hand, was completely detached and floating between my joints, which caused my knee to lock up and create intense pain.

If I was going to have this operation, I knew I would need a goal and something to motivate me during rehab following the procedure. It was already a big blow to know my quadricep, hamstring, and calf would totally atrophy during the six weeks' non-weight-bearing period. I needed to have a reason to fight back.

Durango has a cycling event every Memorial Day weekend that races the Durango-Silverton train. The fifty-mile road race climbs over Coal Bank Pass and Molas Pass, both 10,000 feet elevation, where my injury occurred. It would be icing on the cake if I could physically ride my bike all the way to Silverton following my surgery, but more importantly, over Molas Pass—the perfect symbolism that I had physically overcome my injuries. It was November, and the race was in May. I explained my lofty goal to my surgeon, and he encouraged me, saying it was possible to rehab and train in six months.

I had the surgery, and shortly after was back on crutches, working full-time, and, of course, back in physical therapy. As soon as I was given the clear by my doctor, Jon and I started spin classes again. To my surprise, my muscles came back more quickly and stronger than ever. The reality was, yes, my muscles had atrophied, but this time around, my nerves weren't damaged, so when I started training, my body responded much better than before.

I woke up the morning of the Iron Horse with a bundle of nerves in my stomach. I was excited, scared, and anxious all at the same time. No one was making me race, but I knew I had to at least give it a shot . . . and I am so glad I did! I can honestly say that before my accident, I wasn't in the physical condition to ride my bike from Durango to Silverton over those massive climbs. But now I was in peak physical condition and stronger than before my accident. The race took everything in me, but I finished in great time and with the biggest, most victorious, smile on my face.

During the lowest points of my recovery, I never would have imagined, and no one could have convinced me, that I would one day be able to complete the Iron Horse. I have now completed it twice. And the race has been that much sweeter and brought more praise from my lips *because of* the depths of my despair and the valley from which I crawled. Only God brings beauty from ashes (Isaiah 61:3).

10.

Healing

Durango was a place of physical healing for me. I'll always be grateful for the medical care I received, the beautiful and rugged terrain of the mountains that encouraged my physical therapy, and our community of friends. I knew that though I had one lingering injury, God was still in control, and I had reason to rejoice.

Time passed after the Iron Horse, and my health was stable. We had now been married for seven years, and life was practically perfect. My real estate career was taking off, and I had just been recognized nationally for my work in *REALTOR® Magazine's* "30 Under 30" issue. Jon's job was going really well too. We loved each other, our work, and our friends in Durango. We also had just built and moved into a new home and were finally starting to talk about having children.

You know how life goes, though. Just as we were getting

comfortable, we started sensing that some of our family members were struggling both physically and economically. It was 2009, the peak of our country's economic crisis. After being so heavily supported by our families for the years following my accident, we didn't feel right about kicking our feet up and enjoying our current blessings. So we began to pray about whether or not there was any way we could help.

God has a funny way of answering those kinds of prayers. As we continued to have conversations with our families and each other, we began to feel a tug to move back home to Kansas, if only for a season. And then one day, we both—almost *simultaneously*—received the same call:

Go serve family.

It was crystal clear. As much as we loved Durango, we knew God wanted us back home to help our families.

You'd think if we both heard this call that we'd be excited to move, but we were hesitant. Yes, we loved the idea of living closer to family and being a part of everyone's day-to-day life. We had missed out on a lot living so far away. But we had also created a foundation for our own family in Durango. We wanted to be grateful for—and *present in*—our jobs, especially given the economy. I had built my client base and was ready to be catapulted to the next level. Wouldn't it be foolish to leave and start all over again now?

Healing

"No," God said. "Walk away."

I was also anxious about reconnecting with past relationships back home. Enduring the trials from my accident had changed me. I didn't know how to relate to old friends since I had gone through such a huge transformation. In Durango, people were used to what had happened to me; they saw me through the details. Back home, I still felt a bit like a stranger, even though I was known so well by so many.

We decided to make the move and, within two weeks, found a home in Lawrence and a tenant to occupy the house we had just built in Durango. The next thing we knew, Jon was working full time, and we were living back in our hometown.

To be honest, life in Kansas was about as difficult as I feared it would be. The move did, in fact, prove to be a death sentence to my real estate career. I couldn't find a job with the economy the way it was, I had no clients to help me create one, and I didn't have the energy to start over, so instead, I found myself helping my brother start a dental practice. I loved working with him, but I became bitter that I had lost the career I worked so hard for.

The relationships I feared also proved to be difficult. When asked simple questions of "How are you?" or "What have you been up to?" I couldn't sum up my accident quickly, so my initial reaction was to try and avoid people. Or sometimes I would downplay the seriousness of it all or even pretend it didn't happen. I had always taken great pride in the fact that I was emotionally and physically strong. I didn't like to show my weaknesses, so I kept everything inside. No one at home besides family really knew the extent of what we had been through, so I began to feel very misunderstood.

What I *hadn't* expected in our move was to step into new trials almost as emotionally devastating as my accident. There is no way God would allow that, right? About the time we moved back, my mom unexpectedly went through a divorce. She had remarried after my dad passed away, prior to my accident, and my stepdad had been a huge advocate for me throughout my medical journey. He loved and treated me as his own daughter, so it hurt to sever our relationship. My grandfather, who had been more of a father figure in my life than a grandfather, also became ill shortly after our move and passed away.

And finally, my biggest heartache. Children. I was twenty-seven when we moved back to Kansas, and Jon was thirty-one. At the time of my accident, having children was the furthest thing from my mind, and I punted that worry down the road. During the seven years I spent in and out of the hospital, agonizing over physical therapy, and praying fervently for healing, though, I watched friends get married and have a baby a year later. And then it seemed as if they would get pregnant again and again, easily. *In time,* I kept telling myself. *Once I am healed, we will have the time and energy for children.* I only assumed Jon and I would have the same luck as our friends once we were ready.

By the time we made it to Kansas, we were longing for children, but I couldn't get pregnant. As we continued to receive negative pregnancy test results month after month, doctors ran multiple tests and began telling us we might not be able to get pregnant, or that it would at least be "very difficult." I began fearing how my body would respond carrying the weight of a child if I was even able to get pregnant and became concerned for my own health as well as the health of a baby if we conceived. The last thing I wanted to do was risk the health of an innocent baby because I so desperately wanted to be a mom.

"When are you going to have children?" people asked us frequently. It was a natural question since we had been married so long, but I had no response. I wanted to scream back, *"We are trying!"* Harmless other comments like, "You will understand when you are a mom," and going to baby showers cut deep. I wanted to be happy for my friends, but I was envious instead. *Why, God, are you making us wait for children?* I wondered. *What about the dream I had so many years ago? Forget having* children! *Can't we just have* one?

Over time, as one trial piled on top of another, my

heart hardened. In my mind, we were being obedient and making sacrifices in our life to "Go serve family." Why would God not bless our effort? And what did "Go serve family" even mean anyway? I was trying to help my mother through her transition and assist my brother with his practice, and meanwhile, Jon was being pulled in the *opposite* direction to work for *his* family. We were spending virtually no time together. I remembered the days we were teammates—even the painful ones when I was in the hospital!—and wished we could go back. No more daily life together, no more working toward the same goals, and no children of our own. Our call to "Go serve family" seemed to be at the expense of our *own* family, the one we were trying to create.

I became very angry with God. I would go through the daily motions of faith, but the intimacy I had developed with him throughout my recovery was lost. God had clearly called us to go back to serve, and we knew we were right where we needed to be. *But if I can't see the fruit of our labor,* I wondered, *what is the point?* Where was my reward? My attitude made our time at home almost unbearable.

What I didn't understand, or wasn't able to see at the time, was that God *had* put me in a position to bless me. Blessing just wasn't the immediate action I was expecting or hoping for. It wasn't a baby nine months after our move. It wasn't a seamless family life or the same skyrocketing career. God's blessing came in the form of healing I didn't even know I needed. Not the healing of my body—he had already performed miracles there! The healing of my heart, my mind, and my very sense of self.

When God put me in the unexpected position at my brother's dental office, he began restoring relationships, starting with the one I had with my brother. Our relationship was one I didn't even realize had drifted over time. God also healed a lot of my relationships with members of my Kansas community—friends of my family who I had lost touch with after losing my father. Most of my brother's patients were old family friends and past patients of my dad. God used my time working with my brother to reunite with these friends and give me a greater sense of gratitude for how they supported our family during a tragic time.

Watching my mom go through a divorce taught me probably my greatest lesson. She had gone through such pain enduring the loss of my dad and becoming a widow, and now she suffered a divorce. Yet, I couldn't fully understand how she felt. As much as I loved her, I was still fairly limited as to how far I could enter into her pain. Suddenly I realized how much I had expected others to fully understand *my* pain after my accident. But how could they? The pain was mine, and God had called me to rely first on *him* for compassion. Others were simply called to walk alongside me as best they could. The Lord taught me I had to let go and forgive hurt feelings I didn't even know were there. I had to stop dwelling on my past and the things I had suffered and refocus on the blessings and miraculous work God had performed in my life. I also had to take my eyes off my own desires and start empathizing more with those around me.

It was gentle—the way God worked. He showed me through my daily interactions in Kansas that I had created a void after I left home. Not only had I "moved on," but I had also become very focused on my own hurt after my accident. It was unintentional, but I had lost sensitivity to the fact that people around me were struggling with their own trials. As I reengaged with these loved ones, God used our relationships to heal me emotionally.

Slowly but surely, I learned that my time in Kansas *wasn't about me.* I wasn't in Lawrence to re-establish my career or be a mom or even "save the day" for the loved ones in our lives; I was there simply to bless others, put myself aside selflessly, and truly *serve.*

* * *

Jon and I continued to walk down the unknown road of having children for three years. Day after day, we clung to hope even though a pregnancy seemed impossible.

Because we believed that God knew the desires of our hearts and had given us the desire to have a family, we made Psalm 37:4 our mantra: "Delight yourself in the Lord; and He will give you the desires of your heart. Commit your way to the Lord, Trust also in Him, and He will do it" (NASB). We continued to pray. We consulted with doctors to assess the risk and believed the blessing for our obedience was coming.

Finally, ten years after Jon and I were married, we found out we were pregnant—with not one, but *two* baby girls. I can't explain the awe I still have today as I remember the dream God gave me so many years before our happy news. God used our babies to give us hope for the future and allowed the pregnancy to go smoothly. Pregnancy was actually the best I have physically felt, and Ava and Alex were born perfectly healthy. I am so very grateful for the everlasting joy God has lavished on our lives through them.

When the girls were three months old, God opened a door and called us back to Durango. All of the pieces fell easily into place: our house was still waiting upon our return, I was able to step right back into real estate, and Jon was offered his job back. An added bonus was that my mom decided to move back with us. It was difficult to leave, but serving our family was going to look different now; Jon and I needed to take care of our children.

It's been a joy to watch and learn from my mom as she interacts with her granddaughters, and I am so happy to see her fully restored and receiving God's abundance alongside us. "Instead of your shame you will receive a double portion. And instead of disgrace you will rejoice in your inheritance. And so you will inherit a double portion in your land, and everlasting joy will be yours" (Isaiah 61:7).

My one lingering injury when we moved back to Durango was my drop foot. I had come to a place, though, where I had stopped striving. I was finished complaining and wondering and working to be fully healed. For too long I had tried to achieve healing on my own and merely given God "fist bumps" as I had another successful surgery or accomplished another physical goal. When healing didn't come, though, I would secretly be disappointed with God and wonder what I had done wrong. Now that I was back home and a mother to two beautiful girls, I wanted to revel in a new season of life and not let my accident hold me back. I had seen enough of God's healing; I believed sufficiently in his grace and power.

About that time, I was referred to a new foot surgeon and encouraged by multiple doctors to explore the possibilities of one last surgery to correct my drop foot. I was hesitant to try it because so many other procedures had failed. *God has been so good to me lately,* I was practically thinking. *I don't want to be disappointed in him now . . .*

Still, I remembered what I believed God had promised me so long ago. *Full restoration. Complete healing.*

I decided to have the surgery, and now, I no longer have drop foot.

I wish I could say that my full and complete healing—and it has been *full* and *complete*—has allowed me to master faith and confidence in God and his power. I would love to say I never doubt him, and I believe 100% every day in his promises for me. The reality is, though, I still struggle. I know that faith can be easy for me one day and very difficult the next. Why? Because life is hard, and I'm human, and it's my nature to strive and try to achieve and "recover" out of my own flesh and pride. It is *not* my nature to rely on God and give him the glory he so rightly deserves.

True emotional, spiritual, and physical healing *does* come when we stop striving, stop operating in our flesh, stop trying to prove ourselves or control our outcome. But we're only able to do this—we can only let go of the reins, submit, and give God control—*by his power and grace.*

If I could sum up the most difficult and glorious lesson I've learned in my journey of healing, it would be this: God never promised us an easy life. In fact, he told us to expect the opposite. "In this world you will have trouble . . ."

"*But*" he says. "Take heart! *I have overcome the world.*"

(John 16:33).

I have spent the last fourteen years of my life reflecting back on my accident on Molas Pass and unexpected journey home. It has been an obstacle course of discovery: hoops to jump through, unexpected twists and turns, face plants in the mud. Just when I think I'm understanding what God is up to, he surprises me. He teaches me something new about myself. Gives me the eyes to see someone else. Reminds me I have very little in my control. In and through it all, I have seen how his ultimate providence has allowed everything to happen in his perfect timing. He has tested and challenged me and used his creation to help heal me. God worked through the doctors and nurses to give them wisdom on how to best treat me. He worked through family and friends to encourage and support me in *all* areas of my life, not just my accident. He brought specific people into my life along the way and created divine relationships. He wove me together with everyone I have come across to get me where I am today. And now, *because* of the trials in my life and God's faithfulness in the midst of those trials, I can live at peace with a joyful heart because I know that no matter what the Enemy tries to use to harm my family or me, God will always prevail. As stubborn and sinful and human as I am, I have learned that life is not about me; it is about giving God glory and being his instrument to use as he sees fit.

Healing

For so long I thought my physical healing was the most miraculous thing God had done in my life. Now, though, looking back, I see how he's done so much more. The Lord has healed my body, restored broken relationships, given me the gift of children, and most precious of all, deepened my relationship with him and called me to greater dependence on him. I can now say with confidence: "Consider it pure joy, my brothers and sisters, whenever you face trials of many kinds, because you know that the testing of your faith produces perseverance. Let perseverance finish its work so that you may be mature and complete, not lacking anything" (James 1:2-4).